What's the Catch?

How to Avoid Getting Hooked and Manipulated

By David Sobel, M.D.

Illustrated by Jeff Jackson
Foreword by Robert Ornstein, Ph.D.

HOOPOE

Hoopoe Books
A division of
The Institute for the Study of Human Knowledge

HOOPOE

Published by Hoopoe Books
a division of The Institute for the Study of Human Knowledge
The *All About Me* series is part of the Human Nature Program of ISHK

Copyright © 2010 by The Institute for the Study of Human Knowledge
Illustrations for *What's the Catch?*, copyright © 2010 by Jeff Jackson

Foreword by Robert Ornstein, Ph.D.

General Editors: Denise Nessel, Ph.D., and Robert Ornstein, Ph.D.

978-1-933779-78-2

What's the Catch?
How to Avoid Getting Hooked and Manipulated

Contents

Educational standards covered by this book (*see end of book*):

    APA National Standards for High School Curricula

    CA Middle School and High School Health Standards

    CA State High School Life Science Standards

    National Board for Professional Teaching Standards - Health

    National Board for Professional Teaching Standard: Adolescence and Young
       Adulthood Science

Acknowledgements

Some years ago a social psychologist named Robert Cialdini wrote a book called *Influence* (now in its 5th edition). This college textbook distilled the science on how people can be influenced and manipulated. Why wait for college to learn about influence? For years, family counselor Sharon Scott has developed a useful approach called Peer Pressure Reversal to help teens be able to say no, and still keep their friends.

As teens, you are young adults and you need to learn how people around you, the media, and your own thoughts and feelings guide, shape and control you. And you need to learn the vital skills on how to avoid unwanted or undesirable influence.

This book could not have been completed without the help of Robert Guarino, the author of two other books in this series: *Me and My Memory: Why We Forget Some Things and Remember Others* and *Me and My Feelings: What Emotions Are and How We Can Manage Them*. Robert brought his experience as a high school teacher to the task ensuring that the text and examples chosen to illustrate aspects of influence were relevant.

Foreword
Open During Remodeling

Now that's a sign you don't see very often, and for good reason. Ask anyone who has had to live in a home while remodeling was going on in the kitchen or bathroom. Most businesses just close up shop while the place is being torn up and put back together. Remodels are messy, disruptive and downright inconvenient. But that's exactly what's going on in your brain!

There was once a time when all the changes that occurred around puberty were blamed on hormones. Now, we're not letting the surge in chemicals through your body off the hook, but today scientific research reveals that a second growth spurt in the brain also contributes to the changes that occur during the teenage years. Surprisingly, the changes to a teen's brain are similar to the growth of a baby's brain in the first eighteen months of life. A massive spurt of new brain cells called gray matter occurs, and nerve cells called neurons make new connections. Then slowly, throughout the teenage years and into the early twenties, cells that don't make connections are trimmed back.

Scientists speculate that this second growth spurt aids us all in adapting to the world. It seems this is the last chance in life to learn a new skill or develop a lifelong habit easily. If you take up a new skill or keep practicing at an old one, your brain will rewire itself to support these abilities at a faster rate than at any other time in your life. No wonder the teen years are such a good time to take up playing guitar or drum, or to learn to speak Chinese or Italian! On the other hand, you want to avoid getting into some bad habits because these get wired in, too, and will be harder to change later on. Now is a really good time to learn some good habits for dealing with anger, stress, and self-control. Good habits learned now really could last a lifetime.

First, you should know that the brain's frontal lobes are responsible for self-control, judgment, organization, planning, and emotional control. These are skills many teens struggle with in middle and high school as this part of the brain matures. And, according to research conducted by Jay Giedd[4] at the National Institute of Mental Health using Magnetic Resonance Imaging (MRI), a number of additional unexpected brain developments occur in people from ages 10 through mid-20s. This altered the previously held belief that a person's brain was fully mature by ages 8 to 10. MRIs first revealed that the corpus callosum, the part of the brain that connects the left and right hemispheres, continues to grow until a person is in their mid-20s.

While the implications of this are not fully known, the corpus callosum has been linked to intelligence and self-awareness. Elizabeth Sowell of UCLA's Lab of Neuro Imaging[*] found that the frontal lobes of the brain grow measurably between ages 10 and 12. The gray matter in the lobes then begins to shrink as unused neuron branches are pruned. Studies such as these continue at different research centers, and a more complete understanding of what this all means is around the corner.

While this brain remodel has its rewards, getting through this time in your life can sometimes feel very complicated and you struggle to make sense of the world around you. Maybe you find yourself wondering why you're suddenly so concerned about what others think. Maybe you find yourself wanting more privacy. Or maybe you're just trying to understand why you have to learn algebra!

New questions. New school. New styles. You're changing. Your friends are changing. But you might be able to make more sense of these changes if you have the right information.

---

[*] See http://www.loni.ucla.edu/~esowell/edevel/pub.html for a list of some studies on MRI studies.

I'm not talking about the flood of information on cable TV, radio, or the bijillion blogs and websites on the net. I'm talking about "big picture" information about what it means to be you: a human being. It's information so fundamental, we often forget to teach you about it in school. For example: What psychologists know about how we see, think, and feel; how these abilities work, how they change, grow or get stuck and how reliable they are as we try to make sense of ourselves, our friends, our relatives and the world around us. There is good, solid information readily available and scientifically validated, but a lot of people seem to be too busy to pay attention to it. It's like an open secret. And it's all about you . . . and me.

So, the next time you feel like you are struggling to crawl out from under the rubble of your remodeling, try to remember how great it's going to be when it is all done. Better yet, take an active role. Use the open secrets discovered in this book and others in this "All About Me" series as your hammer and nails to build the you that you choose to be. In the meantime, enjoy this journey - it's all about you!

Robert Ornstein, Ph.D.
President, ISHK

3

Sharon

The new girl

Frank

The Web "browser"

Marquis

The punchline

Sally

Wants to fit in

Jillian

The critical thinker

Esteban
Easily swayed

Ron & Ivy
Saying "No"

Kyle & Camel
Party animals

Jane & Melanie
The popular girls

Dee & Tanika
Best friends

Tanya
The price checker

The Cast

Often appearing and some supporting characters in this book

The concepts in this book just can't be described without some good visuals, so here are some characters who will help to illustrate the uses of influence covered in this text.

1

10 FREE CDS FOR THE PRICE OF ONE ($15) *

Getting Started

An online music CD club offers you 10 free CDs for the price of one ($15). This seems like a great deal compared to $150 if you bought all 10 CDs. But by doing so, you are obligated to buy 4 more CDs at regular club prices ($20) over the next year. You end up spending over $100 and buying some that you really don't care for after all. (Chapter 2)

Alice was approached in a store by an attractive cosmetics salesperson who offered her a free makeup lesson that would enhance her "unusually beautiful eyes." Alice ends up 15 minutes late for lunch with her mother after having spent more on eye makeup than she had ever dreamt possible. (Chapter 3)

Gary needed to cram up for tomorrow's history final and was making his way to the quiet of the library when a group of students he really wanted to get to know rushed up to him: "Come on, man! Don't you know it's the last chance to buy tickets for this show; they're selling out fast. We're all going," said one. Gary, who had not thought of going to the show before this, welcomes the chance. (Chapter 7)

Stephen's uncle Jack was a policeman and his favorite uncle. "All the kids from that school are delinquents, you want to avoid them at all cost," he said as they drove past the Crestwood School. But Stephen knew that Brian went to that school and so did Luke. Could they be the exceptions, or was there something about them he didn't know? (Chapter 6)

Melanie, Jane and Suzie were the most popular by far. All the girls looked up to them, and Wendy was really proud to be invited to their party. Since the party was on a school night, she'd have to tell her parents that she was staying over with Mary to work on some project, but it would only be a white lie. (Chapter 7)

In all the above examples, people were influenced to think, feel or behave in ways they might not usually do. Sometimes influence is helpful, but at other times we end up shortchanged. We will explore these examples, and many others, as we try to help you be more aware of the forces nudging and pushing you. Once you are aware of these forces, you can learn how to choose and protect yourself from unwanted and unhelpful influence.

Let's say you are watching some fish in a pond. A small bug lands on the surface of the water. Instantly a large-mouthed fish zooms to the surface and snatches its dinner. Gulp! The fish didn't ponder its moves. It just acted instinctively. The response triggered by the insect dancing on the water is an **automatic response** wired into the nervous system of the fish. Thoughtful, deliberate, hesitant fish would probably starve.

Another fly appears on the surface. The fish zooms in, gets his dinner and a hook. The fish got more than he bargained for. It got hooked. The fisherman understood the **instinctive** (automatic or **preprogrammed**) behavior of fish. He used this knowledge to trick the fish and catch his own dinner.

In some ways we are all fish swimming in a giant pond. We are surrounded by messages from the environment that trigger automatic responses, both behaviors and feelings. Most of the time, these automatic responses lead to good things. But all too often we can be manipulated and influenced by those who want to control us, sell us something, or get us to do something.

In this book, we'll look at how people (from parents to peers) and media (from advertising to the internet) try to influence us. In order to get the most of out of this book, you should participate in the "Try This" and "Your Turn," etc., activities scattered throughout the book.

By understanding your own reaction patterns, you can avoid getting hooked. You can learn to see more clearly when you are being helped and when you are being manipulated, brainwashed, and tricked. You can also learn when and how to protect yourself from unwanted influence.

2

The Comparison Effect:
What Just Happened?

(U) TRY THIS

Stand in a doorway with your palms facing towards your sides. Now press the backs of your hands hard against the immovable sides of the doorframe. Keep pressing. Hold it for at least 15 seconds. Now step forward out of the doorway. What happens to your hands? (You have to get up and try this, not just read about it!)

(?) WHAT'S GOING ON?

Our nervous system is wired to respond to things based, in part, by comparing the current experience to what just happened before. Your arm muscles, used to pushing outward on the doorframe, continue to press even though now they meet no resistance. The absence of resistance compared to the previous immovable force of the doorway feels positively light and your arms float upwards. Similarly, if you are outdoors in the cold for some time and enter a warm room, the room may seem hot by comparison. Our perception of what is happening to us or around us is influenced or changed based on what just happened before. This is known as the **comparison effect**.

10

⚠ YOUR TURN

Sit in front of three buckets of water: one with hot water, one with ice-cold water, and one with room-temperature water. Put one hand in the hot water and one in the cold water. After about 30 seconds, put both your hands in the room-temperature water. Even though both hands are in the same bucket, the hand that was in the cold water now feels as if it is in hot water, while the one that was in hot water now feels like it is in cold water. The perception of temperature in each of our hands is influenced by its previous experience.

DID YOU KNOW?

Sometimes the comparison effect can be a matter of life and death . . . at least for frogs. An old experiment looked at what happens when frogs get into hot water. If the frog is dropped into a pot of boiling water, it will sense the heat and immediately jump out to safety. However, if the frog is put in warm water, and the water

11

is slowly heated, the frog doesn't notice the slowly increasing heat. It just feels a little bit warmer because the frog's perception is influenced by how it felt just before. As the water slowly reaches boiling, the frog, unfortunately, well . . . croaks. Don't try this one!

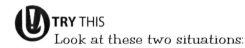 **TRY** THIS
Look at these two situations:

1. Your teacher comments that the class did very well on an assignment, the students might expect to get an A. You then actually get a B on the assignment. How will you feel about your B? Most people will feel sorely disappointed with a B grade when compared to the expected A.

2. Your teacher instead says that just about everyone in the class did poorly on the assignment with the average grade being a D. Again, you get a B. How do you feel this time about your B? Most people will feel very relieved and pleased.

WHAT'S GOING ON?

The comparison effect operates in many areas of our life. While it is most obvious when making physical comparisons like in the experiment judging hot and cold, we also use it to judge our own achievements or success. Your reaction to the same grade (in this case a B) depends on what came before, your expectations of an A or a poor grade.

TRY THIS

Write down a brief explanation for the following scenario: The basketball star Kobe Bryant averages about 30 points a game. He scores 20 points and the fans are disappointed. A lesser-known player scores a career high of 20 points; it is considered spectacular. If they both scored the same number of points to help the team, why do the fans react differently?

Share the above scenario with a friend or relative and ask him or her to explain why the fans react differently.

WHAT'S GOING ON?

Once again, we see the comparison effect operating to judge success or achievement. In this we are comparing a person's current performance to how he or she performed in the past. If Kobe Bryant is expected to score 30 points, a 20-point game -

13

in comparison - is not considered good. It is so common to judge this way that most of the time we are unaware we are making these comparisons. You can see this in the explanations of your friends and relatives. They may not have used the phrase "the comparison effect," but they probably understood why the fans were disappointed in Kobe Bryant.

TRY THIS

Reconsider the example above where you received a B on a test.
1. How would you feel if the top student in class received a C?
2. How would you feel if students who routinely score D or below received an A?

WHAT'S GOING ON?

You have seen that our assessments are influenced when we compare results to expectation or results to previous accomplishments. In this example, comparing our performance to others around us influences our assessments. In the example above, most people will feel good about their B if an A student scored lower, but you probably won't feel good about the very same B if D students scored higher than you.

It is a good idea to become aware of how the comparison effect influences your judgment - especially when we compare ourselves to others. Sometimes these assessments are just not fair to us. In an extreme example, if I compared my baseball skills to Derek Jeter, I may never want to play baseball again! I should more realistically stick to comparing myself to men my own age and ability. Do you ever find that you are comparing yourself unfairly to the brightest student in class or the most talented student in an art or music group?

YOUR TURN

Make a list of typical skills or qualities that interest teenagers. For example: good at baseball, singing, nice eyes, nice hair, good reader, and good at math. Try to come up with at least 10 on your own. Now rate your success in these categories from 1-5 stars (with 1 being the lowest score and 5 stars being the highest).

When you have finished rating yourself, try to figure out why you gave yourself the rating that you did. Are you allowing expectations to influence your rating? Are your ratings influenced by previous accomplishments? Or are you comparing yourself to another person? Finally ask yourself: "Are my comparisons fair or reasonable?"

In 1954, social psychologist Leon Festinger[2] proposed the theory of **social comparison**. This theory states that we compare ourselves to others in order to evaluate our opinions and desires. The group we choose to compare ourselves to is called our **reference group**.

There are two main types of comparison: **upward social comparison** and **downward social comparison**. In an upward social comparison, we compare ourselves to a group that we consider better in some way. In this type of comparison, we look for similarities in our views. This makes us feel better about ourselves: our opinions and desires. When there are differences between the group and ourselves, we may feel like we don't fit in. We may become concerned that the group may dislike us. There may be pressure to change our attitudes and conform, or else face rejection.

In a downward social comparison, we compare ourselves to a group that is less fortunate than we are. If we receive a C on a test, we compare ourselves to those that received a D or F and consider ourselves better off than the others.

A study demonstrating the effects of group membership on political views was begun in 1935 in Bennington College, Vermont.[8] At this isolated college, the older students and professors were liberal, but the majority of incoming freshmen were from very conservative families. There was a wide gap in the attitudes of the new students and their reference group - the older students.

Over the four years in college, the conservative students changed their attitudes and became more liberal. Whereas 62% of the freshman class characterized themselves as Republicans, only 15% of the senior class were Republican. Even after 25 years, most of these students were still politically liberal.

Many of the reference group changes that we make in high school and college become important for life. There was no coordinated effort to change the Bennington students' attitudes. A lasting and substantial change occurred because of social comparison.

⚠ YOUR TURN

Write in a journal or notebook about your feelings towards a group that is not your own. What is your opinion of them and why? What influencers are involved in your opinion. Are you interested in finding out whether you are correct, and, if so, how will you do so? If not, why not?

Another reason we make comparisons are for our self-enhancement. This is basically when you say to yourself "I did better than x." For example, if you get a B+ on a test and Mario only got a B when he often gets the same grade or better than you for his work, you feel better about your grade. This works for evaluating our social standing or our place in our society as well. At the end of a group recital, your school group might deduce from the very loud applause they receive that they are the best and most popular group at the event. People in business might aspire to becoming among the top 10% of wage earners, and when they do so, they feel that they "have arrived" or "made it."

(U) TRY THIS

Write about a time when you found yourself thinking: "This is a total disaster" or "I really screwed up this time."

? WHAT'S GOING ON?

Bringing the comparison effect to your rescue may help you gain perspective. If you did screw up and cause serious problems, that's one thing, but many times we tend to exaggerate the situation, making a molehill into a mountain, a minor embarrassment into a major disaster.

You might ask yourself, "What difference will this make next week, in a year, or in ten years?" Will anyone remember (let alone care) that you made a stupid remark, spilled food on your sweater, dropped the ball, or any number of common slip-ups? Another comparison is to ask yourself how big a deal this would seem when viewed from a satellite circling the earth . . . that is, compared to all the other problems in the world.

MORE FUN

Try doing something nice for a classmate or parent? You can give a small gift, a sincere compliment ("You are very smart, beautiful, strong," etc.) or even a funny joke. Would you think that a small, simple act of kindness, a bit of good luck, or a good laugh could influence how the other person thinks about himself or herself as well as others?

DID YOU KNOW?

When people get gifts, stumble on some good luck, no matter how small, or when they laugh, it usually boosts their **mood** (that is, their longer lasting feelings). And when people are in a good mood, the comparison effect can work to their advantage: the problems seem smaller. When they are more satisfied with their classes, teachers, classmates, friends, their own appearance, and

19

so on, problems, in comparison, can be kept in a better perspective. They are less likely to turn a molehill into a mountain.

This **mood swing**, however, only lasts for a short while, so you have to try to find the small things throughout the day to boost your outlook and the moods of those around you.

ⓤ TRY THIS

Imagine that you are going shopping for a new T-shirt. You see the same shirt you like in a different store. One store is selling the T-shirt on sale for 25% off; the other store is selling it as - "Buy one at regular price and get a second one for 50%!" Which deal looks better in comparison? Which is actually a better deal: a T-shirt on sale for 25% off OR buy one T-shirt at regular price and get the second for 50% off?

WHAT'S GOING ON?

Advertisers and retailers often try to influence us by using the comparison effect. In the above situation, the second option may seem to be a better deal. We seem to be getting two T-shirts at a greater discount of 50% off vs. 25% off. However, if we take the time to do the math, we realize that in both cases we are paying the same amount for each T-shirt. In the first instance, we are paying 75% of the original price. In the second instance, if we divide the 50% savings by 2 shirts, we are paying . . . 75% of the original price per shirt. What seems to be a better deal for the consumer is actually a better deal for the retailer who has now sold 2 shirts instead of one!

A similar process occurs when people and media try to influence us. Stores are forever having sales. An "originally priced at $19.95 - now reduced to $9.95" seems much more appealing than the *same* item priced at $9.95 but not on sale. The tendency is to compare the sale item with the price that it was *before* the sale.

YOUR TURN

Look through the advertisement section of a newspaper or take a trip to a local shopping area. Take note of how often retailers use the comparison effect to make their sales look more attractive.

Beware of Mail Rebates

Your friend wants to buy a portable DVD player. The regular price is $100, but he can get a $20 rebate, so he figures he's actually paying a discounted price of $80. A good deal by comparison.

Perhaps you should remind him that this is true only if he actually mails in the rebate coupon. Nearly half of the people do the discount calculation in their heads but *never bother to mail in the rebate coupon!*

Have you ever bought something that had a mail-in rebate coupon? Did you mail it in and get a check back *and* cash it? If not, you got hooked.

HOOKED

Consider the following example: Let's say you walk into a store to buy a pair of shoes priced at $79. After buying the shoes, the salesperson shows you some cool T-shirts for only $15 each. After just spending $79, $15 dollars doesn't seem like much, and you go for a T-shirt, too. You took the bait! If you just walked in the store and only saw the $15 T-shirts, research suggests you would be less likely to buy one.

AVOID THE HOOK

If you understand this automatic comparison effect, you can avoid getting snagged. For example, when you are about to buy something, ask yourself four questions:

1. How is the true value of the item determined?
2. What am I comparing the item to or what did I expect?
3. What happened just before this and could it possibly be affecting my decision?
4. Do I need more time before I make this decision?

Above all, be aware of what you are comparing things to, *especially in light of whatever just happened.*

Sometimes the best way to defend against comparison is to delay a decision. Buy some time. Think it over. If you are not comparing something with whatever just happened or came before, you are more likely to make up your mind with less influence or distortion.

Have you ever really wanted something - perhaps a new cellphone, computer, or even a new boyfriend or girlfriend? You might have told yourself that you can't "live without it." And let's suppose it was something you did not get. Chances are that within a few days, or weeks, you may have forgotten about it all together, or at least survived, and probably wouldn't think it was as important. Delaying and buying some time can really relieve the pressure of the comparison effect.

Key Ideas in Chapter 2

Our nervous system is wired to respond to things by comparing the current experience to what just happened before. This is called the

comparison effect. Advertisers, retailers and our own friends and family often try to influence us using the comparison effect. We use the comparison effect on ourselves, too, to judge our own achievements or success.

Our **mood** also affects our choices. When people are in a good mood, the comparison effect can work to their advantage making problems seem smaller.

The two main types of comparison are (1) **upward social comparison**, where we compare ourselves to a group that we consider better in some way and (2) **downward social comparison**, where we compare ourselves to a group that is less fortunate than we are. The group we choose to compare ourselves to is called our **reference group**, and many of the changes we make in high school and college which are based on our reference group become important for life.

 *KEEP IT IN MIND*

Now you have an idea of how the comparison effect works, try to use it to your advantage. Find small things to do throughout the day to boost your mood and make a note of them, so that you remember what they are and can use them in the future.

When you do face problems, you can keep them in perspective by remembering and using the strategies we have discussed in this chapter.

Another technique you might try is to think of a time in the past when you were unhappy. Now compare that to your present situation. Using the comparison effect, how do you think that might change your mood in the present? By comparison, would you likely be happier or sadder? Maybe your current problems don't seem so bad after all.

3

Give and Take: IOU

Have you ever seen a waiter or waitress bring a mint or candy with the bill in a restaurant? This is not unplanned or an accident.

Which of the following actions would likely get a food server in a restaurant a larger tip:

  a. Places a bowl of mints by the exit door of the restaurant

  b. Leaves no mints with bill

  c. Leaves a single mint for each diner with the bill

  d. Leaves two mints for each diner with the bill

  e. Leaves one mint but then quickly returns and leaves another mint for each diner

❓ WHAT'S GOING ON?

Would you think that a mint or two could influence you to leave a larger tip? Well, most customers swallow the "bait," even if they don't swallow all the mints. In the example above: 'e' increased tips by 23%, while 'd' increased tips by 14%, and 'c' increased tips by 3%. The bowl of mints by the door comes after the customer has paid the bill and so has no influence on tips.

When someone gives us something, from advice to money, we feel obligated to return the favor. Psychologists call this the **reciprocity rule**. We may not even be aware of the tendency, but as a rule we are influenced by anyone who gives us something. We don't know why, but this seems to be as strongly wired in us as our need to respond when someone asks us a question.

Oh boy, oh boy!

FREE

The reciprocity rule tends to be more powerful when the "gifts" appear significant (two mints work better than one), unexpected, and personalized. Notice this in the example 'e' above, where the server returns "unexpectedly" and leaves the gift of a second mint "just for you." This has a greater influence than bringing the same two mints for each diner with the bill.

YOUR TURN

Look through a newspaper or go shopping with a parent or friends and make a list of how many advertisers or retailers offer "free" merchandise. This has become a very popular strategy in grocery stores. They often give free samples or tastes of products. You might be surprised at how much this boosts sales. After accepting the free sample, people tend to feel obligated to buy some more, *even if they did not particularly like the product*!

DID YOU KNOW?

"Free" often equates in people's minds with $0.00, which doesn't seem like it is very valuable. Therefore, which ad is more attractive?

- or -

Calling out the worth of the item ($200) puts the emphasis on the value of the gift. Linking the MP3 player to one's favorite music also helps to strengthen the personalization of the gift.

The reciprocity rule or principle has been studied by anthropologists, economists, sociologist, and psychologists. Anthropologist Bronislaw Malinowski[6] called it the **principle of give and take**. Sociologist Georg Simmel[12] referred to it as "gift exchange." In 1971, psychologist Dennis Regan[10] conducted an experiment in which he examined reciprocity as a tool of influence.

Regan's subjects thought they were taking part in an art appreciation experiment. They were accompanied by an accomplice who they thought was another subject, and they were both asked to rate the quality of paintings. The experiment took place under two different conditions. In some cases, the accomplice did the subject a small favor, such as bringing the subject back an unsolicited soda. In other cases, the accomplice did not do a small favor for the subject.

Later on, the accomplice said that he was selling raffle tickets and would win a prize if he sold the most. Regan found that the subjects who got the small favor bought twice as many raffle tickets as those for whom no favor was done. Clearly the subject who bought more tickets felt obliged to do so.

More interestingly, this experiment revealed that it does not matter whether or not you like the person who did you the favor. At the end of the experiment, subjects filled out questionnaires in which they were asked whether or not they liked the accomplice. Those who received a favor repaid the accomplice with more ticket sales - even when they answered that they did not like them.

TRY THIS
Sometimes the "gift" comes in a strange form. Ask your friend to borrow $25. Let's say he or she says no. Then ask him or her if you could borrow just $1. Chances are your friend will say yes.

WHAT'S GOING ON?

Two things. First, you have influenced your friend's decision using the comparison effect: $1 seems small in comparison to $25. Second, you have just done your friend a favor and given him/her a gift of sorts by reducing the request from $25 to $1. You have made it easier to say "yes" and not feel badly.

Using a strategy of a "larger-but-then-smaller" request usually gets the other person to comply. (Remember, after the end of this experiment, tell your friend what you were doing and you can both learn from this experience. You can also immediately return the $1 as another gift.)

Sales people do this routinely to hook the customer. When entering a store, they will often show you the most expensive product. If you buy it, fine. If you don't, they show you a less expensive version that "will save you a lot of money" and seems by comparison to be a much better deal. This sales technique combines both the comparison effect (the less expensive item seems like a bargain) and the reciprocity rule or gift-giving effect (the salesperson just did you a favor by showing you the less expensive item and *saving you big bucks*!).

Many advertisements try to get you to send for a "free, no obligation" information packet or sample. In accepting this offer, realize that you are also likely to trigger a sense in yourself that you should buy more or sign-up for the whole package - even if you don't especially like the offer! Once hooked, your response may have more to do with the gift **reflex obligation** than with the value of the product and service.

⚠️ YOUR TURN

Talk to parents or older relatives and make a list of all the "free gifts" they are offered. If they need help getting started, find out if they have ever been offered a free trial subscription to a magazine. Dentists like to give patients free toothbrushes. Even military recruiters will offer high school students free posters.

🙂 MORE FUN

Get together with a few friends and try to recall all the free gifts you've been offered. Remember the toys you received in those hamburger meals or in breakfast cereals?

HOOKED

Consider the following example: You receive a "personal invitation" from a local department store that you have shopped in recently inviting you to a special sale. Just show a salesperson the letter and you will receive additional discounts. If you go on this unplanned shopping trip, you took the bait.

Notice that this invitation uses the strategies of the reciprocity rule. The invitation was unexpected, the additional discounts seem significant, and it is a *personal* invitation to a *special* shopper. Refer to Chapter 5 for an additional "secret" to the power of this sales technique.

AVOID THE HOOK

With both fish and humans, there seems to be no free lunch. This doesn't mean you should decline all gifts and favors. To defend yourself from unwanted influence, be careful when accepting free gifts in the first place. Accepting the gift or favor unconsciously obligates you to return the favor (even if you consciously say it's no big deal). Here are four good ideas on how to avoid the hook:

1. **Just Say No:** If accepting the gift puts you in an uncomfortable position, then graciously decline.

2. **Look for the Hook!** If someone offers you a free sample (soft drink, candy, anything), ask yourself why the giver is giving you something. What is their hidden agenda or reason? If you feel that someone is manipulating you with the gift, then accept it but recognize the act for what it is - a trick, not a favor. Tricks do not trigger the same reflex obligation to return the favor.

3. **Buy Time:** If you do accept a gift, then at least delay responding to the favor. With time you may figure out the motive behind the gift, and then you can make a clear-headed decision about whether to return the favor.

4. **Return the Gift:** Sometimes it may even be necessary to return the gift.

Key Ideas in Chapter 3

When someone gives us something, we feel obligated to return the favor, even if we do not like the person or the freebie. This is called the **reciprocity rule** or the **principle of give-and-take**. Advertisers, retailers, solicitors of all sorts, and our own friends use this principle to hook us into doing or giving more than we really wanted. By recognizing this hook, we will be able to know when to say no, or buy time, or return the gift, and we will not be making **reflex obligation** choices without thinking.

 *KEEP IT IN MIND*

Don't think that all gifts are bad. There are many gifts that we can be grateful for. For example, a birthday gift from grandma or a pat on the back from a close friend when you are feeling down is a genuine gift. Think for a moment and then write down 3 things you are grateful for that happened in the past day. It can be anything . . . a good grade, a new music track, a compliment, playing with a favorite pet, an accomplishment in sports, etc. How did this exercise make you feel? Just concentrating for a moment on things we are grateful for can usually make us happier.

Try doing this same simple exercise at the end of each day for two weeks. Just write down 3 to 5 things you are grateful for. Research shows this can improve mood, not just when you write but throughout the day as you search for the good things that happen. It also helps balance out some of the daily stresses and hassles.

Remember to distinguish genuine gifts from those that are designed to influence or even manipulate you.

Mirror, Mirror:
We Buy What We Like

TRY THIS

Imagine that three people come up to you and ask for a favor. One person is a close friend and classmate. The other is a stranger your age but from a different school. And the third person, asking for the same favor, is a classmate you do not particularly like. Which person are you likely to do the favor for, and why?

WHAT'S GOING ON?

People tend to say yes to people they know and like. It is very difficult to turn down a request from a friend, or even from someone who just appears to be friendly. When a friend, relative, or a neighbor who you like asks you to buy something (from candy bars to magazines), the chances are you will. You'll do it, even if you don't like the candy, cookies, or have subscriptions to 16 magazines that you don't read already. We are much more likely to be influenced to make the decision to comply with a request from someone we like or admire.

TRY THIS

Think of people who you like. Make a list of all the reasons why you like them. Ask a friend or relative the same question and see if you can't add to your list.

WHAT'S GOING ON?

If you are like most people, you'll see from your list that we seem to like people who are similar to us, or flatter us, or cooperate with us. In addition, you may be surprised to learn that we seem to be **programmed** internally to like people who are more physically attractive.

TRY THIS

Let's say you need to hire someone to do a job for you. Look at the three portraits below. Let's say they are equally skilled and qualified to do the job, but you can only select one. Which one would you choose?

WHAT'S GOING ON?

Studies show that good-looking people seem to have an unfair advantage. Good-looking job applicants are more likely to get hired than even more qualified, but less attractive candidates. Handsome workers get higher salaries. Does it surprise you that studies show people are more likely to vote for physically attractive candidates in elections? All this may not be fair or as we would like it, but we assume unconsciously that good-looking people are more intelligent, more capable. Scientists suggest that this **bias** (a bias is a "one-sided" attitude) may have evolved in prehistoric times. According to this idea, unblemished skin, symmetrical facial features, and a well-proportioned body signal good health. Selecting a healthy mate would, in those days especially, increase the chance of producing healthy children.

Advertisers are aware of this bias. Ever notice how the people in most ads are cuter, younger, and more vibrant than the average person on the street? We are more likely to change our opinions or be influenced to buy products when pitched by an attractive person. Good looks sell, whether we like it or not!

DID YOU KNOW?

Just as we are more likely to say "yes" to someone who we like or to someone who is similar to us, we are also more likely to agree with or buy something from someone who we perceive as similar to us in opinions, personality, background, or lifestyle. Studies show that people are even more likely to help other people who are dressed similarly to them! You are more likely to buy something from someone who is similar in appearance, who goes to your school, or who comes from your hometown than from someone quite different.

It is for this reason that organizations - from the military, to colleges, to trade schools - try to send a high school alumnus to campus to recruit for them. These organizations know that your decision can be influenced by someone who you perceive as similar to you.

⚠ YOUR TURN

Go to a library and look through magazines. Try to determine the audience that the magazine is trying to appeal to by the way people are dressed in the advertisements. You can conduct similar research by channel surfing and paying attention to commercials. For some obvious differences, compare the commercials on *Nickelodean* to a so-called women's channel like *Oxygen* or a so-called men's channel like *Spike*. How would the differences in appearance mirror different target audiences?

⚠ YOUR TURN

Let's say you are looking for a new pair of shoes. You go into Store A and Store B:

In Store A, the salesperson says: "The shoes you are trying on are really terrific. They are very well made. I really like the cool stitching along the sides. The cushioning makes them very comfortable to wear. I found that they also last a long time."

In Store B, the salesperson says: "Wow, what a coincidence! Those shoes you are wearing are the same ones I have at home, but I like the color you got them in better. Which one of these other shoes do you like? Maybe I can get a pair too."

So, which store are you more likely to buy from, A or B? Which sales pitch is likely to be more effective and why? We may like to think of ourselves as people making rational decisions and choices based on the quality of the product alone. In practice, other more emotional and personal interactions often influence our decisions. Skillful sales people will often try to emphasize their familiarity and similarity to you: quickly referring to you by name, complimenting you, identifying things you may share in common, etc.

? WHAT'S GOING ON?

We respond positively to compliments and flattery. Even if we consciously dismiss it, if someone offers us a compliment about anything (attractiveness, clothing, intelligence, etc.), we are much more likely to be persuaded by that person. We tend to like people who seem to like us.

We also tend to like people and ideas like ourselves. We are unconsciously drawn to people and things that remind us of ourselves. People driving similar cars often nod or honk at each other. Research has even shown that people with the name Johnson are more likely to marry Johns, and women named Virginia are more likely to live in (and move to) a Virginia state. And people whose name is Lane tend to have addresses that include the word "lane," not "street."

TRY THIS

Type your first and last name into a Google search, and chances are that you will find many other people with the same or similar name. A new word has been made for this: "Googleganger" derived from "Doppleganger," which means double.

WHAT'S GOING ON?

Surprisingly, you are more likely to feel a positive connection with people who have similar names even though they are complete strangers.

DID YOU KNOW?

When you nod your head "yes" or shake your head "no," you are not just influencing others. You are influencing yourself! An Ohio State University research study demonstrated that simple movements influenced people's agreement with an opinion they heard.[9] Without our being aware of it, nodding or shaking our head communicates to ourselves how we feel about our own thoughts. When we nod "yes," we gain confidence in what we are thinking; when we shake "no," we lose confidence in our own thoughts or opinions.

This doesn't mean that you will agree with whatever you hear if you are nodding "yes." It's more complicated; if you approve of what you heard, nodding will increase your positive opinion. On the other hand, if you disapprove with what you've heard and nod "yes," you will increase your confidence in your negative thoughts on the subject. Similarly, if you are shaking your head "no" while listening to an opinion, you will lose confidence in your own ideas on the subject. Shaking your head "no" influences you to doubt your own thoughts.

Other body movements, such as writing with your non-dominant hand (left hand if you are a right-handed), can also influence your attitudes. In another study, research participants were asked to write down three good qualities they had with respect to planned careers. When interviewed afterwards, participants had more confidence in their thoughts if they wrote them with their **dominant** vs. **non-dominant hand**.

When questioned afterwards, participants said they did not think body movements influenced their answers. Researchers suspect that we are unaware of influencing our thoughts and attitudes with a whole range of body movements we have, including smiling. Yet our bodies speak our minds.

TRY THIS

Think back to a time when you were watching a sporting event with someone rooting for the other team. If you are not a sports fan, try to find someone who is, or else try to remember a time when you may have observed a group of sports fans. Now imagine that a foul takes place, at least you think so, but your friend from the other school or team insists it wasn't a foul. What usually occurs? Would you be surprised if an argument breaks out?

WHAT'S GOING ON?

Many of us are devoted fans of sports teams - from professional teams to school teams. We feel a sense of loyalty to defend "our" team, and this sometimes leads to seeing reality completely differently. Well, some researchers actually studied this by showing some films of a football game to students from the two different competing schools. Students were asked to note if they saw any penalties or instances of cheating. What the students

41

saw depended upon which school they were from. In their eyes, the opponents always committed more fouls and penalties than their home team.

People tend to seek out information that agrees with their own biases or beliefs. People who smoke will screen out messages about the serious health effects of smoking, whereas people who are against smoking seek out information that supports their point of view. The same is true in politics where people seek out information about candidates to fit their biases. Liberals seek out blogs and news sources that support their views, while conservatives take in a steady diet that reinforces their views. Once again, we can see that we are more likely to be influenced by people who are like us or have similar ideas as we do.

TRY THIS

Make a list of all the celebrities or athletes who you can think of and the products they endorse. Ask your friends and relatives to help you add to your list. Finally, search magazines or watch TV commercials. Can you list at least 20 celebrity-endorsed products?

WHAT'S GOING ON?

Perhaps the strongest influencer is when people we like (or don't like) are associated with products or ideas. Advertisers compete to associate their product with beauty, strength, fame and fortune. Sports stars and popular entertainers are paid to link themselves and endorse products related to their sport (sport shoes, athletic clothing, sports equipment, etc.) or their music (CDs, stereo equipment, etc.). Some stars even sell their bodies as live advertising billboards with tattoos of **branded products**!

But celebrities are often found endorsing and promoting completely irrelevant products, from soft drinks to detergent, from games to vacations. What special knowledge of cars does a baseball star have? Why should we believe a leading pop vocalist when she gulps down a soft drink? If I drive this car or drink that drink, will I be more like the celebrity? We are not just buying the product, we are buying the association. We take the bait.

We want to connect and be associated with winners, the rich and famous. When our sports team wins, we usually shout, "*We won! We're* champions!" However, when our team loses, we distance ourselves and mutter, "*They* blew it. *They* lost."

⚠ **YOUR TURN**

Now, review the previous list you made of celebrities and endorsed products. Which celebrities might actually know something important about the product? For example, a basketball player might work on the special design of a new shoe and his/her opinion might be relevant. But which celebrities are seemingly mismatched and the paid endorsement is just that - a purchased pitch?

TRY THIS

The next time you watch a TV show or movie, see how many brand names and products you can spot. The Apple Computer? The Ford Explorer? The Nike Shoes? The Coca-Cola? Perhaps you can have a competition with a friend to see who calls out the product first or how many total branded products you can identify.

WHAT'S GOING ON?

With more and more people skipping TV commercials with digital video recorders or using the commercial break as a signal to go to the bathroom or refrig, advertisers have turned to **stealth marketing**. Look at the list of brand-name products you made - a computer, a portable music player, a soft drink, a car, a box of cereal, etc. Well, the chances are those products did not show up by accident in the movie or TV show. The maker of the product probably paid a lot of money to the movie producers to display their product prominently. This is called **product placement** and it is a form of stealth marketing. The goal is to expose you to the product and link it with an enjoyable, entertaining experience. What kind of car does James Bond drive? What candy does E.T. like?

Today we are bombarded not only by obvious advertising, commercials, and billboards but by a much more subtle form of advertising. We are increasingly surrounded by ads and endorsements, some of which are harder to detect and, therefore, harder for us to defend against. Companies are purchasing the rights to rename sports stadiums. Guests waiting to appear on the talent-contest hit show, "American Idol," are shown waiting in the "Coca-Cola Red Room." The world is becoming a giant billboard.

Companies are weaving their products into the actual story-lines of soap operas and television shows. The animated movie "Foodfight!" features brand name products such as Twinkie the Kid, Charlie the Tuna, and Mr. Clean as characters. Drug companies are paying celebrities to discuss prescription remedies on TV talk shows. Marketers give expensive athletic shoes to popular, trend-setting students to influence their classmates. Actors are hired to pose as tourists asking people on the street to take their pictures with the latest cellphone/digital camera technology. Once the device is in the person's hands, he or she often asks, "Where can I get one?"

When you search on the internet, many of the "hits" or links are actually paid advertisements, not objectively rated sources of information.

When you watch a commercial or view a print ad, you at least know someone is trying to sell you something. With stealth marketing, you are being hooked and you don't even know it.

TRY THIS

Divide up into debate teams with several people on each team. The teams can include classmates, friends, or family. Pick a topic. It can be some issue from the news, politics, or a topic like: Should school kids wear uniforms or anything they want? Is the illegal sharing of downloaded music actually wrong? First start with people taking the side they most believe in, then switch sides. Those in favor now have to argue the other side and those against need to speak in favor. When you have finished, ask everyone how easy it was to switch sides? Did you find the arguments as compelling or interesting? Did people argue as forcefully?

WHAT'S GOING ON?

Most of us desire to be consistent and to maintain our commitments. Once we have made a commitment or taken a stand on an issue, we struggle to remain consistent. Therefore, it should not be too surprising to find that it is difficult to argue an opposing opinion with the same energy and interest. Just as we associate and identify with people we like, we come to identify ourselves with certain ideas and causes.

We tend to like people like ourselves, and we tend to like ourselves when we are most consistent with our ideal of ourselves. For example, if I consider myself a generous person and then catch myself behaving in a mean way, I won't like myself. Our desire to maintain a consistent identity can also make it easier for others to influence or manipulate us.

In most circumstances, consistency is a valued **trait** (a "trait" is a characteristic of someone's personality). People who are inconsistent are often thought of as scatterbrained, weak willed, or unreliable. Similarly, we value commitment. Many romantic novels include characters who remain committed to loved ones long after they are dead. We admire heroes who remain committed to their causes even when facing defeat.

Because these traits are often valuable, we often act automatically. We try to maintain a consistent attitude or approach *even when it is not in our best interest.* In 1966, psychologists J. Freedman and S. Fraser demonstrated this in an experiment in which they asked homeowners in a residential neighborhood to allow them to install a public-service billboard on their front lawn.[3]

In this experiment, "volunteers" approached homeowners, made the request, and showed them a photograph. This "sample" photo showed an attractive house almost completely out of view behind an ugly billboard that simply read DRIVE CAREFULLY. The majority of the approached homeowners (83%) rejected the idea of putting an ugly billboard on their front lawn. But one group of approached homeowners overwhelmingly (76%) accepted the idea!

Why would a group of homeowners agree to a request that was not in the best interest of keeping their front lawns looking good?

The reason is that these homeowners were behaving consistently to a commitment they had previously made. Two weeks before the billboard request, a different "volunteer" had visited this group of homeowners and requested they display a three-inch square sign that read BE A SAFE DRIVER. Because they had been willing to comply with this relatively minor safe-driving request, these homeowners (76%) were primed to comply with another request which required a much greater sacrifice.

Freedman and Fraser conducted another experiment to test the **theory of consistency and commitment**. This time, prior to asking homeowners to put an ugly billboard on their front lawn, they sent "volunteers" to a select

group and requested they sign a petition which favored "keeping California beautiful." When the second "volunteer" returned to the homes of those who signed the petition, approximately 50% of these homeowners agreed to place the same ugly "Drive Carefully" billboard on their front lawn. Freedman and Fraser found this result even more significant because the previous commitment these homeowners made was NOT to driver safety, but to an unrelated topic. They concluded that once the homeowners agreed to the first request, their attitude of themselves had changed. They acted consistently as the kind of person who takes action for a good cause - *any* good cause.

These findings suggest that agreeing to trivial requests increases our **compliance** (going along when someone asks us to) with very similar, much larger requests. But, we can also be influenced to perform a larger favor that may not be directly related to a previous trivial request.

These conclusions are supported by scientific studies of American prisoners of war (POWs) during the Korean War in the 1950s. Upon their return to the U.S.A., many were evaluated so that scientists could understand why the Chinese were able to get many of these men to cooperate and publicly denounce the U.S.A. One finding that emerged was that the Chinese captors did not immediately force the POWs to comply with large requests. Instead they first manipulated them to make small, seemingly trivial concessions. These small acts of compliance influenced the POWs to change their view of themselves and their captors. In time, the Chinese captors were able to make larger requests of the POWs such as making statements critical of the U.S.A. Many of the POWs would comply for the same reason that homeowners complied - in order to remain consistent.

—HOOKED

Consider a time when you or a friend just had to have something that you saw endorsed by a favorite celebrity or athlete. Maybe it was a camera or a pair of shoes. Maybe it was simply the latest sports drink or snack. If you rushed out to get the product or bugged your parents into submission, then you took the bait.

So, how can you protect yourself from the unwanted influence of how much you like people? The answer lies not in rejecting others or acting inconsistently, but in observing the effect on you. Here are two ways to avoid the hook:

1. **Observe and Challenge:** If you find yourself liking someone (salesperson, celebrity, or acquaintance) more than you might have expected, that is a clue that you may be vulnerable to being hooked. For example, if you find yourself wanting a certain product because a celebrity promotes it, you might try to separate the person from the product? Ask yourself, how well do I really know the person? Is he or she qualified to recommend the product? Is he or she paid to recommend the product? And, finally, how good is the product and do I really need it? If you can separate your feelings about the requester from the request, you have a chance to avoid getting hooked by unwanted influence on your decisions.

2. **Explore the Other Side(s):** To understand our own beliefs and biases, especially when they are about people, poverty, or race, we need to expose ourselves to a broader range of information from diverse sources and points of view. For example, if you have negative feelings about homeless people, then volunteering at a shelter or soup kitchen will expose you to real people in this situation . . . and you may find that you and they are not so different after all. Though we may favor

and seek out those like ourselves, we may also discover new insights and understandings by reaching out to others in our diverse community.

△ **YOUR TURN**

Write in your journal or notebook about a visit to a different environment and meeting different people. For example, if you helped at a homeless shelter, did this experience change your previous opinions about the homeless? What do you think the influencers were that affected this change in your opinions?

Key Ideas in Chapter 4

We are unconsciously drawn to people and things that remind us of ourselves. We seem to like people who have names like ours, or flatter us, or cooperate with us. People make many major choices by seeking out information that agrees with their **biases** or beliefs.

51

Agreeing to small requests (or **compliance**) increases our chances of agreeing with much larger requests because of our need to be *consistent*, even if these choices do not serve us well. We can avoid reacting to our biases by challenging ourselves on our choices, separating our feelings about the requester from the request, and by reaching out to others not like ourselves.

Advertisers select well-known personalities with whom we identify (and hope to appear like). They associate their product with beauty, strength, fame and fortune, even if these attributes have nothing to do with the product. Popular TV, sports and movie personalities are a favorite tool for these advertisers, who use tricks such as **stealth marketing** or **product placement** to make sure we associate the product with our favorite personalities.

 *KEEP IT IN MIND*

The philosopher Ralph Waldo Emerson wrote, "[a] foolish consistency is the hobgoblin of little minds..." Set yourself a weekly goal to explore the diversity of opinions and ideas. It can be anything from eating at an unfamiliar restaurant to reading a book that you initially dismissed as "not your style."

And remember, signing a petition or getting involved in one good cause doesn't commit you to get involved in every good cause. Consider your options and prior commitments.

5

Scarcity:
Wanting What We Can't Have

The Friday after Thanksgiving is known as Black Friday. Many stores use that day to launch their end-of-year holiday shopping season. To attract people into the stores, they open early (some at midnight!) with "door busting" special offers. "An iPod at 50% off for the first 20 people." "A special laptop computer for $15...while supplies last." Many people camp out the night before and wait hours for the doors to open (watch out, some people have been trampled). Though hundreds may show up lured by the prized limited-quantity bargains, very few actually get them.

TRY THIS

Look through your daily newspaper or take a trip to your local shopping center. How many retailers are offering sales "for a limited time only"?

WHAT'S GOING ON?

"Hurry, last two items available! Don't miss out." Just adding words like this to an ad can increase how much we want and value something. We are afraid of missing out on good deals. And we don't like anything standing between us and what we want. When something is common and easily available, there is little urgency to try to get it. However, when we think something is rare or scarce, we rush to possess it. Special, one-of-a-kind items are particularly tempting. The **scarcity phenomenon** is also one reason that prices often go so high when people are bidding against each other at auctions (including eBay!).

When things appear scarce (even if they are no better than what is equivalent and easily available), we want them more. Scarcity triggers an emotional reaction which can cloud our judgment and influence decision-making.

⚠ YOUR TURN

Conduct some long-term research. Look through your daily newspaper for a couple of weeks and compare the total number of ads using the scarcity phenomenon during the week to the total number of ads using this influence technique on the weekend. Graph your findings.

Extend your research if a major holiday is approaching. Compare the number of ads using the scarcity phenomenon on a non-holiday week-end with ads using this influence technique on or near a holiday weekend.

☺ MORE FUN

Conduct some research on eBay. Choose any three items, perhaps a videogame or handbag or a football jersey. Track the listings of these items for a week or so. Try to determine if there is a pattern to the amount of time each type of item is left up for auction. Are most MP3 players auctioned for 72 hours? Is it best to leave a piece of jewelry up for 96 hours?

Before beginning any internet search, be sure to get the permission of your parent or guardian. Also review Chapter 8 "Caught in the Net: Don't Get Hooked Online."

Ⓤ TRY THIS

Do a brief interview with someone who collects things like stamps, coins, trading cards, comic books, dolls, wine . . . anything. Ask him or her:

○ How do you know if something is truly rare and **collectible**?

○ How do you determine the value of what you collect?

○ Have you ever been fooled into thinking something is rare, and it turns out not to be? What was it, and why do you think you took the bait?

○ How do you think you can protect yourself from being fooled?

○ How could you make a common object seem rare and special?

WHAT'S GOING ON?

Collectors of rare objects are especially vulnerable to the scarcity tactic. The perception of scarcity is what makes these objects collectible. But watch out for copies or fake collectibles as well as what is called the **precious mistake**. These are "flawed items" - a blurred postage stamp, for instance. A stamp carrying a three-eyed likeness of George Washington is highly sought after and quite valuable. These types of valuable collectibles do not come around that often.

Yet, sellers use the term quite often when offering anything they want to sell us. They merely call the object a "collectible" and jack up the price. We should take a lesson from a popular antiques TV show appraiser who advises that when the word "collectible" is used, it doesn't mean the item is rare or valuable. It simply means the seller wants you to "collect" it at whatever price they set.

Sellers or retailers use other scarcity tactics to influence your purchases. Sometimes we fall for the **limited-number principle**. Anytime a retailer advertises a limited number of items on sale or promotes a sale "while supplies last," the retailer is using the limited-number principle. If merchandise is advertised as being limited in number, it may or may not be true since the only intent of the marketer is to convince customers of an item's scarcity - the retailer is often not bothered with the truth!

Have you ever seen an ad for several items and one of them has a stamp across it saying "SOLD OUT"? What does that do to your perceptions of the remaining items still for sale?

Then, there's the deadline tactic with an official time limit and expiring date: "One-Day-Only Sale" or "Buy now, these shoes will not be here after 4 o'clock!" Will they be walking out on their

own . . . or something? Probably not - someone will take the hook, and that's what the seller is counting on. Many times it's these advertisements themselves which are anything but scarce! There is one department store that advertises a sale in the newspaper nearly everyday ("The One-Day-Only Sale," "The Day Before the One-Day-Only Sale," "The Day After the One-Day-Only Sale," etc.). It seems the only sale they miss is "The Only Day of the Year We Don't Have a Sale

Day!" Popular online auction sites such as eBay take advantage of the deadline principle. As the end of the offer approaches, you can observe increased bidding at increased prices.

A common retail practice used by auto dealerships is known as the **loss leader**. This tactic combines the limited-number principle with the deadline tactic. In this case, the dealership advertises a particular model car at a very low price. In the fine print, it is revealed that only one or two cars will be available at this price and only for one or two days. The name "loss leader" refers to the fact that while the retailers will often lose money on a particular item, they have succeeded in leading many people to visit their stores in pursuit of this rarity.

Sometimes scarcity itself arouses our interest. Lotteries thrive on the thought that one could win a million dollars, even if the chances are one in 10 million.

⚠ YOUR TURN

Turn your junk mail into something useful for a week or two. Organize a contest with a friend or two to see who can scavenge for the most advertisements that use scarcity tactics. Put them aside and tally them up at the end to declare a winner.

If you find it difficult to find ads in your junk mail, include looking through a local newspaper. The Sunday edition works best as it usually contains the most ads.

DID YOU KNOW?

In basic economics, the scarcity phenomenon underpins the **principle of supply and demand**. If supply is greater than demand, the price goes down. If demand is greater than supply, then the scarcity phenomenon influences the price, and it goes up.

On a daily basis, this can be seen in the energy market. When a natural disaster or war disrupts the flow of oil and limits supply, the price of gasoline increases. But this limit can be artificial, too: the organization OPEC purposely influences the price of oil by increasing or decreasing the amount of oil they sell.

This principle can also be seen when new electronic devices are introduced. At first, when supplies are limited, the devices are expensive. Over time, the prices fall dramatically as the supply increases. Consider that in 1998 the average PC computer cost just under $1,300. In 2010, the average PC computer costs $400-$500 and is much more powerful. Some websites even track and provide graphs of products over time. Usually they go down in price, except when they are truly in short supply or out of stock.

TRY THIS

The next time you have a conversation with a friend or family member, and he or she seems distracted and you are having trouble getting his or her attention, try this: Suddenly say in a hushed voice, "I am going to tell you something that only a few people know, but you have to promise not to tell anyone." Observe that person's reaction. Do you get his/her full attention? Does he or she lean forward towards you? Do his or her eyes suddenly focus on you? That is the power of a secret - it can influence others' attention.

59

WHAT'S GOING ON?

What is a secret? It's some information which is kept hidden from others. You may know something that others don't. This specialness and scarcity give secrets some of their power. We all want inside knowledge. It give us access to exclusive, rare information.

Again, advertisers may use secrets to grab your attention. Coca-Cola contains a secret formula. Secret ingredients pepper many products. And censored, forbidden or restricted items or behaviors often have so much attraction.

Not only do marketers use these tactics to force their product on us, but notice how many friends and relations do it to get what they want. If your parent, for instance, tells you that a movie is rated "R" and off-limits to you, don't you feel that your choices are being limited, and doesn't that make you want to see the movie even more? How many friends have said you just *had* to go to a once-in-a-lifetime party at someone's house while their parents were away? Or, perhaps they said you had to try or do something which is taboo, rarely possible and always secret.

People's reliance on scarcity as a tool (or a weapon) of influence is frequent, wide-ranging, and quite inventive. It relies on our weakness for shortcuts. Our brains are wired to respond to our fears of loss, missing out, or being left out. Sometimes this **reflexive emotional response (or reaction)** serves us well (if food is truly scarce, you would rightly be motivated to get enough to eat). But we are led to believe that things which are difficult to get or to do are typically better than those which are easy or safe. And we use this belief to make choices quickly: we make emotional choices because we tend to assume that something scarce and hard to come by is better.

TRY THIS
Ask a parent, childcare worker, or a friend who babysits what happens when you try taking a toy away from a 2-year-old child and say he or she can't have it back. The child may have many other toys available, but it is only that forbidden one which the child wants . . . and wants badly. Or try it yourself with a couple of 2-year-olds, but watch out! Their reaction may be dramatic and very **Loud!**

WHAT'S GOING ON?
There is a theory that whenever our free choice is limited or threatened, the need to retain our freedom makes us want to keep these choices (as well as the goods associated with them). We start reacting to scarcity early in life, even at age two. It is not just the loss of the object itself, but the thought of the loss of our own freedom that riles us up.

TRY THIS
A pizza restaurant was located in a mall surrounded by high-end stores and expensive restaurants. The manager noticed that customers

61

would often stop and look at their menu out front and then walk away. He tried an experiment. He increased the price of his pizzas by 50%. What do you think happened?

? WHAT'S GOING ON?

Sales of pizzas shot up. Yes, by charging *more*, the number of pizzas sold increased. At first, this may seem strange because we assume that lower prices would mean more sales. But in light of the scarcity principle, it makes sense. People often use price to judge the value and quality of something. The high-end shoppers in the exclusive mall thought that a "cheap" pizza must not be very good, but an expensive pizza must be excellent!

More Desirable Cookies

In a recent study, based on Stephen Worchel's[13] research on scarcity, some people were offered expensive, "hard-to-find" chocolate chip cookies which were rated by the marketers as "more desirable." Many of these people became so hooked that they were willing to pay a lot extra to get the cookies. The marketers were very careful not to say "better-tasting cookies." Yet, despite that fact, buyers clamored to get them. The cookies did not taste better, but the excitement of getting these "rare" cookies stimulated people to pay more.

☺ MORE FUN

Form a small advertising team with your friends. Pick a product or a service your team wants to sell and then design a magazine ad which emphasizes the scarcity principle.

Hint: try to incorporate the influence techniques of rare and limited number, collectible, time-limited offer, and deadlines to drive sales.

—HOOKED

We often use price as a way of simplifying the world and our decisions. We too often automatically assume that the higher priced product will last longer, perform better, be more exclusive and more desirable. Sometimes that is true, sometimes not. Why can designer jeans often sell at 5 to 10 times the price of basic denim jeans which may wear as well or better? Have you or someone you know paid more for designer jeans which perhaps already had holes in them or were frayed? If so, you and your friend took the bait.

AVOID THE HOOK

The scarcity phenomenon tells us that the less available a resource is, the more we want it. It's an emotional reaction. We don't want to miss out. So, how can you defend yourself? Here are three suggestions:

1. **Watch for Arousal:** Use your feelings of excitement and arousal to alert you that you may be under the influence of scarcity. Psychologists call this a **reflexive emotional reaction** and it is a powerful influencer. If you start to feel afraid that you will lose out if you don't act immediately, watch out. The next time you are at a "limited-time-offer" sale, let your mind shoot up some warning flags.

2. **Question Scarcity:** When you notice the excitement, ask yourself:

   o Am I being manipulated by messages of scarcity, time deadlines, or secrecy?

   o Is this message really justified?

3. **Buy Time:** Most (but we must admit not all) items promoted as scarce ("time-limited," "hurry," "act now," etc.) are not really part of urgent decisions which require immediate action. If you can, give yourself a little time to settle down and think. You will be pleasantly surprised at how many opportunities fade away into insignificance with a slight amount of wise hesitation and time.

Once these flags are up, you can still make choices, but you will be well protected against making the choices for the wrong reasons - like buying something just because it is scarce or pretends to be scarce.

Remember the cookie buyers? They emphasize an important aspect of the scarcity phenomenon: just because the cookies were more desirable, this didn't make them taste one whit better. When you are confronted with this tactic, ask yourself "what do I want to get out of this item?" If you want a delicious cookie, then make sure the scarce ones are just that - tasty. If you don't know whether the product is what the sellers are saying about it, do a little research to find out what customers who have bought them say about them. If you have to make a quick decision, then go with your warning flags . . . don't buy. Instead, buy the cookie which you already know is good and enjoy eating . . . *and* one which you can get whenever you want, not when a marketer wants you to get it. *Remember, scarce things are not necessarily better.*

⚠ YOUR TURN

Write in your journal or notebook about a time when you were younger and forbidden to do something which you later were allowed to do. Was it worth waiting for? What influencers were involved in this experience?

Key Ideas in Chapter 5

When things appear scarce, we want them more, even if they are no better than equivalent items. This is known as the **scarcity phenomenon**. When an item is labeled as **collectible**, it is highly probable that it's just a gimmick to sell the item at a higher price.

Be wary of **precious mistakes**, too, where an item has been labeled as rare because of a flaw. Other scarcity tactics which sellers or retailers use to entice a customer include advertising a limited number or a dead-line for the sale. Automobile and other retailers often advertise a **loss leader** item at a very low price simply to get customers to come in and possibly buy more.

Scarcity triggers a **reflexive emotional reaction** which can cloud people's judgment and influence decision-making. So, if people use their feelings of excitement and arousal as a signal that they may be under the influence of scarcity, they may be able to buy time to figure out whether something is valid or not.

 **KEEP IT IN MIND**

It's harder to resist the tactics with friends and family. But you're ahead of the game already because you will recognize their tactics of influence, and your warning flags will help you make safer, more reliable choices.

6

Authority:
Says Who?

TRY THIS

Imagine that you have been asked to participate in a "memory and learning" experiment to test the effects of punishment on learning ability. There is a "Learner," the person who has to memorize a long list of words, and the "Teacher," the person who will test the Learner by delivering increasingly strong electrical shocks for every mistake. A professor wearing a lab coat and holding a clipboard asks you and another subject to draw lots. This time, by chance, you get to be the Teacher.

You sit in a room in front of rows of 30 switches, switches ranging from 15 volts (labeled "Slight Shock") to 420 volts (labeled "Danger: Severe Shock") to 450 volts (labeled "XXX"). Each time the Learner made a mistake, you are instructed to flip the next switch and deliver an increasingly higher shock of 15 more volts.

You can't see the Learner sitting in the next room, but you can hear him. The initial shocks are annoying. The professor instructs you to increase the voltage. As the voltage increases, the Learner begins to complain about the shocks. At 90-volt levels you hear some grunts increasing to groans. You hesitate, but you are instructed to continue to increase the voltage. At 150 volts the Learner cries out, "That's all! Get me out of here. Get me out of here, please. Let me out."

You look toward the professor who calmly reassures you to continue to increase the voltage. The experiment must continue and you are not responsible for the results. At 300 volts the Learner expresses concern over his heart condition, begs for release and pounds on the wall in agony and then ominously no longer responds.

What do you think you would do in this situation?

1. refuse to be the Teacher as soon as you heard it involves shocking the Learner

2. deliver shocks up to the point you began to hear grunts and groans

3. increase the shocks until the Learner cried out to stop

4. increase the shocks until you reached the maximum of 450 volts if instructed to do so by the professor

WHAT'S GOING ON?

This experiment was actually done in the 1970s by a psychology professor named Stanley Milgram.[7] No one actually got shocked; the Learners were all actors pretending to be shocked, but the Teachers did not know this.

Almost no one believes that he or she would continue to shock the Learner to the maximum. Before the experiment, Dr. Milgram asked a group of psychiatrists to predict how many Teachers would shock the Learners all the way to the last (450-volt) level. They said less than one in a thousand would go all the way.

What happened? The results will shock you. Under circumstances mirroring the features of a bad horror flick, the typical Teacher was willing to deliver as much pain as was available to give. Nearly two-thirds of the subjects pulled every switch to the 450-volt level despite the pleas of the victim! Further, almost none of the 40 subjects quit their job as Teacher when the victim begged for release or screamed. And, only 22% of the subjects refused to go beyond the 300-volt level. This applied to both men and women Teachers.

A Shocking Experiment

How can this behavior be explained? Was this a freak accident or were the subjects a collection of unusually sadistic people? Unfortunately, the experiment has been repeated with very similar results, and, sadly, the subjects are just like you and me. Normal, healthy people will, under circumstances of social pressure, follow authority and even do the unthinkable. The pressure to conform and obey can be very strong . . . strong enough to overcome our natural tendencies not to want to hurt someone else.

The subjects (in other words, the "Teachers") felt an obligation to the experimenter to continue, although they were volunteers and knew they could leave at any time. The pace of the experiment gave the subjects little time to stop and consider their actions. The experimenter, if necessary, encouraged them to continue shocking and reassured them that it was not their responsibility. But when the researcher told the Teacher to stop the shocks, the Teacher immediately stopped, even if the "victims" said it was ok to continue.

We like to think of ourselves as independent, and many of us pride ourselves on defying authority (especially parents, teachers and elders!). Yet, the evidence suggests that most of us, in most situations, will actually obey the instructions of an authority figure - even if the instructions are potentially harmful and destructive.

Despite its appearance, Milgram's experiment was actually designed to help explain the **theory of obedience to authority**. That is, many normal, healthy individuals are willing to carry out severe levels of punishment and pain rather than go against authority. They do this in a mindless fashion, perhaps, as a kind of decision-making shortcut - the shortcut of putting all responsibility onto authority figures, not on themselves.

DID YOU KNOW?

In another disturbing experiment, psychologist Philip Zimbardo[14] set up a mock prison. Students were randomly assigned the role of "prisoners" or "guards." The guards quickly took on their roles and began to exercise aggressive control over the prisoners who increasingly became passive and submissive. The experiment was supposed to last two weeks, but it had to be terminated after only six days due to humiliation and mistreatment of the prisoners. Remember, they were just college students. For more details on this experiment and its implications, visit the website: **http://www.prisonexp.org/**.

Beyond Experiments

The Milgram obedience experiments were largely designed to understand events like the Holocaust in which millions of people were tortured and killed. Those carrying out the atrocities later often said they were "just following orders." Regrettably, we have learned little from such events because mass terror and obedience to authority continues . . . genocide in Rwanda and Sarajevo, torture in Abu Ghraib prison in Iraq - the list is long.

 **YOUR TURN**

Pick up a newspaper. If you don't get a newspaper at home, look at one online or visit a library for one. Look over the articles and see if you can find any examples of people's obeying authority and hurting others. Prison guards, gang members, even seniors in a fraternity can terrorize and humiliate new pledges.

⚠ YOUR TURN

Conduct a database search on the internet for historical examples of mass terror and obedience to authority. Keyword search: genocide, Rwanda, Sarajevo, Darfur, Wounded Knee, the killing fields, the rape of Nanking, the gulag, Armenian genocide. (Before beginning any internet search, be sure to get the permission of your parent or guardian. As there could be some disturbing events and images on some sites you find, ask a parent or other adult to help you do the search.)

ⓤ TRY THIS

Interview several friends or family members. Ask them the following questions:

- o If you walk into a classroom, how do you know who is the teacher?

- o If you walk into a hospital, how do you know who the doctors are?

- o If you see a football team in a huddle, how do you know who the quarterback is?

Notice that most answers will be similar, and people will give you an answer rather quickly.

⁇ WHAT'S GOING ON?

In nature, animals have bright feathers, strong scent, large horns, and other visible signs of authority. So, this goes back a long, long time in our evolution, and it is not surprising that **status symbols** such as titles, clothing or type of automobile have been shown by researchers to influence our own decisions.

People who have titles from M.D. (Medical Doctor) to CEO (Chief Executive Officer), from professor to "King of Rock," people who dress with authority or who have symbols of authority (from judges' gavels to hot cars) unconsciously invite our tendency to do whatever they say.

All authority is not bad, however, because some people have earned the right to be respected and followed. But not all people with titles or in positions of authority have earned this right. When reacting to authority, we must decide whether we are doing so because of mere symbols of authority rather than to its substance.

 **MORE** FUN

Draw two columns. Make a list of authority figures in your own life and out in the world - from traffic warden to President. In the first column, identify at least 10 authority figures. In the second column identify a status symbol for each authority figure. Is it a badge, clothing, a championship belt? These symbols help you to identify each figure's authority more readily.

Expand your list to include items you might not normally consider status symbols. For example, what is a high-status car? What is a high-status MP3 player? What are high-status clothes?

HOOKED

Consider a time when you or a friend needed to make a purchase. Let's say make-up, clothing, or even a used car. You were having a hard time choosing between several items, so you decide to ask your next-door neighbor's opinion. After all, she is a successful business-woman. You are not exactly sure what her business is, but she drives the nicest car on the block. She makes a recommendation. If you follow her recommendation without any further investigation, you've taken the bait.

AVOID
THE**HOOK**

How can you defend yourself against the tendency to obey all authority? How can you begin to distinguish between good and harmful authority? Here are four good ideas on how to avoid the hook:

1. **Ask yourself: "Is the authority a true expert?"** If yes, what makes you think so? We need to take note whether we are being influenced by simply symbols or by the real thing, a real expert or authority. Be careful, though, remember that a person can be a true expert in one area, but give you advice in another where she/he is not qualified at all!

2. **Ask yourself: "How truthful can we expect the expert to be?"** This will allow us to consider not just the expert's knowledge in the situation but also the trustworthiness of the expert. What does the expert have to gain by your complying with their advice or request? You may know the old saying, "Would you buy a used car (or a CD) from this guy?" This is a good warning flag to apply when in doubt as to whether someone is truly an authority or not. Be wary of experts or authorities who give their advice or requests only in secret. If the advice cannot be shared with others, chances are more likely that it is bad advice.

3. **Ask yourself: "Is the authority suggesting you do something that is, or could be, hurtful or harmful to yourself or others?"** Consider not just the immediate consequences, but what the actions or advice might lead to in the future. If harm is likely or even possible, chances are you should not follow the advice.

4. **Take responsibility:** If someone tells you to do something stupid or harmful, in the end it is your decision whether actually to do it. You cannot just say, "Well, so and so told me to do it." That is not a good excuse for the way you behave.

Key Ideas in Chapter 6

Most of us will obey instructions from an authority figure - even if the instructions are potentially harmful and destructive. Stanley Milgram designed an experiment to help explain the theory of **obedience to authority**, as well as to help understand events like the Holocaust and other atrocities. It showed that many normal, healthy individuals are willing to inflict severe levels of punishment and pain rather than go against authority.

Philip Zimbardo's mock prison experiment showed that normal college students ended up humiliating and mistreating "prisoners." Current events are proving that this behavior is still prevalent today.

The display of **status symbols**, such as titles, designer clothes, and fancy cars, does not indicate authority. All authority is not bad, but we must decide whether we are making our decisions based on mere symbols of authority rather than on substance.

 **KEEP IT IN MIND**

A direct request is a common form of **social influence**: we tend to go along because someone asks us to. Psychologists call this **compliance**. (See the Freedman and Fraser ugly billboard experiment on page 47 for more about compliance.) If the person asking something of us is in a position either to reward us (with friendship perhaps) or punish us (by withholding a paycheck or allowance, for example), we are likely to comply. When the person asking us to comply is a legitimate authority, going along is called **obedience**.

While obedience to authority is a fundamental requirement of organized society, in certain situations, ordinary people like you and me will follow the commands of an authority figure, even when the commands are extreme. Unless we are careful and remember the above points, we take the bait. Above all, we need to remember that each one of us is responsible for our own thoughts and actions.

Peer Pressure:
Everyone's Doing It

TRY THIS

Make a list of your friends. Don't limit it to just friends from school. Choose friends from all the different activities you are involved in. Write next to each name the reasons you have for a being friend with him or her.

WHAT'S GOING ON?

Who are your **peers**, anyway, and why are they so important? Peers are people your own age or close to it and people with whom you are in contact. Usually they are friends and classmates at school or in the neighborhood, but they can also be teen celebrities on TV or the internet. You often share interests, experiences and, perhaps most importantly, decisions with peers. You and your friends make dozens of decisions every day, and you influence each other's choices and behaviors. This is often positive **peer pressure** - it's human nature to listen to and learn from other people in your age group who are often going through the same things as you.

As you get older, your peers play a greater role in your life.

Through school and other activities, it is common to spend more time with peers than you do with your parents, siblings or relatives. You'll probably develop close friendships with some of your peers, and you may feel so connected to them that they are like an extended family.

Besides close friends, your peers include other kids in your grade, neighborhood, church, sports team, or community. These peers influence you by the way they dress, act, and behave, by things they're involved in, and by the attitudes they have.

TRY THIS
Look at the list below. For each pair of items, check off which is "cooler."

Long hair on guys		Crew-cut hair	
Button-down shirts		T-shirts	
Rolling backpack		Backpack with straps only	
Converse sneakers		Sketchers	
A nerd		A jock	
Drinking bottled water		Drinking a glass of water	
A touch phone		Ordinary cellphone	
iPod		CD player	
Xbox 360		Nintendo Gamecube	
Jessica Simpson purse		Coach purse	
Levi jeans		Lucky jeans	
Maybelline makeup		MAC makeup	

Now add some items of your own to the list and pick the cool ones.

OK, so why are some things cool and others not? Why does something which was totally cool suddenly become uncool? Do you think everyone in your school would agree with your choices of what's cool? Do you think teachers, parents, kids in China, etc., would also agree with your choices? If not, why?

Peer pressure to conform can even come from strangers.

WHAT'S GOING ON?

Why do people follow the latest fads? Like it or not, research shows we often behave based on what we see other people doing . . . even strangers. If everyone is doing it, it must be good. Unfortunately, we are often misled by this assumption. Perfectly normal people can make poor choices, and this can lead anyone into some unhappy situations.

Research shows that we often determine what is correct by finding out what other people think is correct. This is called the **social proof principle**. What do you do with an empty popcorn box in the movie theater? Look around, what did others do? If there are empty boxes or trash on the floor, we are likely to think it is somehow OK to dump ours there, too, and we add to the pile.

The lesson here is to recognize that just because everyone is doing it, this doesn't mean it's the right thing. Maybe they are doing it because of false information or bad data, or they are just not thinking . . . and by relying on that, we can make things a lot worse and sometimes even quite frightening.

DID YOU KNOW?

See what could be happening to the number of plastic water bottles you and your friends drink from and so often toss away carelessly.

In the broad expanse of the northern Pacific Ocean, there exists the North Pacific Subtropical Gyre, a slow-moving clockwise spiral of currents created by a high-pressure system of air currents. The area is an oceanic desert, filled with tiny phytoplankton (microscopic plant-like organisms which live in the ocean), but few big fish or mammals. Due to its lack of large fish and gentle breezes, fishermen and sailors rarely travel through the gyre.

But the area is filled with something besides plankton: trash, millions of pounds of it, most of it plastic. It's the largest landfill in the world, and it floats in the middle of the ocean.

The gyre has given birth to two large masses of ever-accumulating trash known as the Western and Eastern Pacific

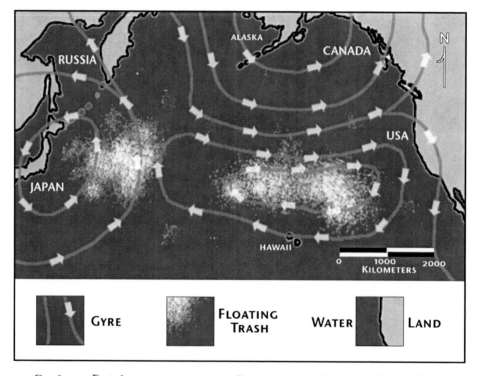

Garbage Patches, sometimes collectively called the Great Pacific Garbage Patch. The Eastern Garbage Patch floats between Hawaii and California; scientists estimate its size as two times bigger than Texas. The patch is characterized by exceptionally high concentrations of suspended plastic and other debris which have been trapped by the currents of the North Pacific Gyre.

What can you imagine would happen to the Great Pacific Garbage Patch, as well as other polluted places on earth, if each one of us considered recycling our plastic bottles in our own neighborhood or school? What would happen if 10 of us did that . . . or hundreds and thousands of us?

While it is common for us to think that peer pressure is something only teenagers face, peer pressure or **group influence** is common for humans of any age and in any society.

A group is not just a collection of individuals; it is two or more people who have a trait, a belief, or an experience in common. Groups influence our behavior through **norms**, **roles**, as well as the group's **cohesiveness** (how "together" the members of the group are).

Norms are the rules of behavior for a group. Norms may be unspoken, but all the group members understand them. Norms exert pressure on an individual to conform or behave as expected. Violation of norms or **group rules** will result in pressure from the group. A role is an assigned task within the group. Again, often we assume roles in a group out of habit or past experience. We may be the leader, the designated driver, the brains, the muscle, or the group clown. As long as we want to remain in the group, norms and roles influence our behavior. The more cohesive the group, the stronger the influence. If a group is not cohesive, then these group or social forces are not effective.

In 1956, Solomon Asch[1] conducted a classic study of social influence on **conformity**. Subjects were not told that social influence was being tested, but rather thought they were involved in an experiment on visual perception. In this experiment, a group of "volunteers" were seated along a table and shown a card with a vertical line. The experimenter then showed them a second card with three vertical lines, one the same length as the first card and two obviously different in length. The volunteers had to choose the line which matched the first.

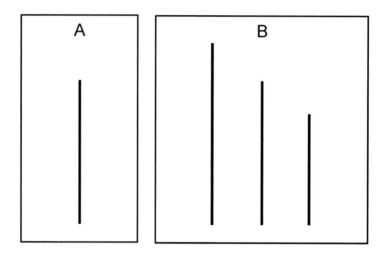

However, each group of volunteers contained only one real test subject and six people who were really the experimenter's assistants. The assistants always answered first and always chose the same incorrect line. The pressure to conform was so great that 37% of the responses given by the real subject were wrong even though the correct answer was obvious. Of course, some subjects never gave the wrong answer, but 76% of the subjects went along with the group at least once and gave a wrong answer!

By conforming, subjects avoided being singled out and rejected by the group. When Asch performed this experiment another time but allowed answers to be written instead of stated out loud, conformity dropped.

Several Factors Determine Conformity

One is group unanimity. When the confederates in Asch's experiment were unanimous, overall conformity was about 36%. If just one assistant did not go along with the others, conformity dropped to only 8%.

A second factor is group size. The larger the group size the more likely we are to conform. In the Asch experiment, only 2.8% conformed when there was only one assistant and one real test subject in the room; 12.8% conformed with two assistants in the room; and 30% conformed with four assistants in the room. In this experiment, conformity was not shown to increase with groups larger than four.

A third factor which influences conformity is a person's relationship to the other people in the group. Conformity increases if we perceive others as experts. When others are seen as unlike us in age, social group or clique, or status, conformity decreases. Our sense of security with others can also influence conformity. We are more likely to conform if we feel insecure within a group.

⚠ YOUR TURN

Stand outside where people are passing by and look up at the sky. Mark down how many people stop and look up and how many just pass by. Now repeat the experiment and have a dozen of your friends all stand looking up at the sky, and count how many people now stop and look up. If many people are looking up, then perhaps others tend to think this is important and they had better look up. Or perhaps they are just thoughtlessly imitating you!

If you walk by two restaurants and one has a long line out front but the other is almost empty, which restaurant would you choose? Likely the one with all the other people (unless you are in a big hurry!). Our mental shorthand says if a lot of people are waiting, it must be a good place. This example also reflects the scarcity principle - if we think something is scarce (or a restaurant is hard to get in), we value it more.

DID YOU KNOW?

Why do most TV producers put canned (or pre-recorded) laughter on sitcoms? Television sitcom executives apply the social proof principle when they decide to use canned laughter on sitcoms. They use laugh tracks for the simple reason that viewers are drawn in by appreciative responses of an audience, hearing others laugh can influence us even if the responses are faked or pre-recorded. It works on us!

Hearing laughter can affect our behavior in other ways . . . whether it is altering an awkward situation, generating more people to laugh, or increasing **apathy** (lack of concern). In one study, participants heard the soundclip of a loud crash in another room and the experimenter yelling loudly enough for the participants to hear it. Upon hearing this noise, participants either came to the room to see what was going on, or stayed in their room and kept doing what they were doing. Ten participants went through this process without experiencing a laugh track. The other ten went through the same process, but they also heard laughter coming from the same room from which they heard the loud crash and yelling. Those who did not experience the laugh track were more likely to help (80%) than those who did hear a laugh track (30%).

It seems that once we hear laughter, we assume that everything

87

is OK. Perhaps our motivation to see what's happening would be to join in on the joke. Some psychologists suggest that the purpose of laugher is to trigger positive feelings in others. Laughter can ease tension and it can be contagious, so it helps to foster a sense of togetherness. Our early human ancestors may have used laughter as a **nonverbal signal** to others that everything was OK and safe.

ⓤ TRY THIS

Ask an older relative to tell you about a time when he or she influenced someone to make a positive choice. It doesn't necessarily have to have been a life-changing experience.

Then ask your relative to tell you about times when he or she can remember being influenced positively by someone else. Did those people ever know the effect they were having on your relative?

Now ask the older relative to tell you about times when he or she can remember being influenced negatively by someone else. Did those people ever know the effect they were having on your relative?

Write in your journal or notebook about your own recollections of being influenced by others to make positive and negative choices. Write about times you might have influenced others to make positive choices.

⍰ WHAT'S GOING ON?

Though you may usually hear about peer pressure as something bad, peers can be very helpful and supportive. Peers can be loyal and fine friends, and friendships made among teens can last for a lifetime. You and your friends inspire each other not only by what you say but by your behavior. And this can happen even without your realizing that you are doing so! For example, your peers can inspire you to do well in school, excel in sports, and help your community.

Sometimes just talking with a peer can help clarify your feelings and help you make a good choice or decision. The decisions may be minor like what clothes look good on you, or major like whether to have sex or to try drugs.

Your friends and peers can also help you learn new skills or explore new activities from sports to music. Sometimes friends can just listen and offer support when things are rough.

Doing what others are doing, as a rule, helps us make fewer mistakes by acting in accordance to what is accepted. We have been living in small groups since the beginning of our history, and this is what makes this influence manipulator so powerful.

Advertisers use this all the time, saying words such as "largest-selling" or "fastest-growing." If others are buying this product, it must be good.

DID YOU KNOW?

In an experiment, a psychologist used our tendency to conform to the group in order to help children overcome their fears.

Children who were terrified of dogs watched as a little boy happily played with a dog for 20 minutes a day. Within only four days, two-thirds of the formerly fearful kids were climbing into a playpen with a dog and cheerfully playing with it. Even seeing a film of other children playing with their dogs greatly reduced the fear. If others are doing it, I can too.

TRY THIS

The following is a list of typical attempts at negative peer pressure:

o "Come on, one small glass of beer won't hurt you."

o "You mean you don't have an iPod! How uncool!"

o "Everyone else is coming to the party. Aren't you?"

o "I didn't get to finish my homework last night. If you are a true friend, you'll let me copy yours."

Talk with your friends and family and try to add to this list. Challenge yourself to come up with at least 5 more examples. If you are stuck, try to recall some examples you may have seen on TV or read about in a short story or novel.

WHAT'S GOING ON?

There is a darker side to following what others are doing. Sometimes the stresses in your life can actually come from your peers. They may pressure you into doing something you're uncomfortable with, such as shoplifting, doing drugs or drinking, taking dangerous risks when driving a car, or having sex before you feel ready.

This pressure may be expressed openly ("Oh, come on - it's just one beer, and everyone else is having one") or more indirectly by simply making beer available at a party, for instance. Once one or two people start helping themselves, many others will do so.

Most peer pressure is less easy to define. Sometimes a group can make subtle signals without saying anything at all - letting you know that you must dress or talk a certain way or adopt particular attitudes toward school, other students, parents, and teachers in order to win acceptance and approval.

The **pressure to conform** (to do what others are doing) can be powerful and hard to resist. A person might feel pressure to do something just because others are doing it (or say they are). Peer pressure can influence a person to do something which is relatively harmless . . . or something which has more serious consequences. Giving in to the pressure to dress in a certain way is one thing - going along with the crowd to drink, smoke or do drugs is another.

People may feel pressure to conform so they fit in or are accepted, or so they don't feel awkward or uncomfortable. Others may go along because they are curious to try something new which others are doing. The idea that "everyone's doing it" may influence some kids to leave their better judgment, or their common sense, behind. When people are unsure of what to do in a

91

social situation, they naturally look to others for cues about what is and isn't acceptable.

The people who are most easily influenced will be the first to follow someone else's lead. Then others may go along, too, so it can be easy to think, "It must be OK. Everyone else is doing it. They must know what they're doing." Before you know it, many people are going along with the crowd, perhaps doing something they might not otherwise do.

Groupthink is the name psychologists give to the type of thinking group members jointly arrive at. This kind of thinking is generally influenced by the perceived necessity to minimize any conflict. No one wants to disrupt what is called the **comfort zone** of the group. The tendency is to want to avoid being seen as foolish by our peers; we are enjoying the feeling of belonging in the group and don't want to be left out, also we want to avoid embarrassing or angering other members of the group.

Because of this, Groupthink may cause groups to make hasty and irrational decisions, where individual doubts are set aside for fear of upsetting the group's balance. This kind of thinking often lacks a proper evaluation or analysis of a situation. This means that, as a group, we may do things which we would definitely avoid as individuals.

To make Groupthink testable, the social psychologist Irving Janis[5] devised eight symptoms indicative of Groupthink:

1. **Illusions of invulnerability** (the group imagines and feels as if it is immune to failure) creating excessive optimism and encouraging risk taking.

2. **Rationalizing warnings** that might challenge the group's assumptions.

3. **Unquestioned belief** in the morality of the group, causing members to ignore the consequences of their actions.

4. **Stereotyping** (making a sweeping generalization about someone, labeling them) those who are opposed to the group as weak, evil, biased, spiteful, disfigured, impotent, or stupid.

5. **Direct pressure to conform** placed on any member who questions the group, couched in terms of "disloyalty."

6. **Self-censorship of ideas** that deviate from the apparent group consensus.

7. **Illusions of unanimity** (the members of the group imagine that they are in complete agreement) among group members, silence is viewed as agreement.

8. **Mindguards** - self-appointed members who shield the group from dissenting or opposing information.

Mindguards play a particularly important role in Groupthink. They actively steer a group away from any information which might cause disagreement. They discourage criticism and limit the range of proposed solutions. Many **cults** which exhibit unhealthy behavior might have been formed by unscrupulous mindguards. Using the chart on the next page, can you match the correct technique of a mindguard with the statement?

1. incomplete survey of alternatives	a. "We just need to do this for the survival of the group/gang."
2. incomplete survey of objectives	b. "We don't have time for more discussion: it's now or never."
3. failure to examine risks of preferred choice	c. "There is no other choice. No other way out."
4. failure to re-evaluate previously rejected alternatives	d. "I checked out all the right-wing opinion leaders and they all agree."
5. poor information search	e. "We only have two choices: you are either onboard with this or not."
6. selection bias in collecting information	f. "There is little that can go wrong with this plan."
7. failure to work out contingency plans	g. "John suggested something else but it won't work and a waste of time to go there again."

Answers: 1 (e), 2 (a), 3 (f), 4 (g), 5 (b), 6 (d), 7 (c)

According to Irving Janis, groups do not have to make bad decisions or fall victim to Groupthink. Janus suggests that groups actively encourage different ideas and opinions. He devised seven ways of preventing Groupthink:

94

1. Leaders should assign each member the role of **critical evaluator**. This allows each member to air objections and doubts freely.

2. Higher-ups should not express an opinion when assigning a task to a group.

3. The organization should set up several independent groups, working on the same problem.

4. All effective alternatives should be examined.

5. Each member should discuss the group's ideas with trusted people outside of the group.

6. The group should invite outside experts into meetings. Group members should be allowed to discuss with and question the outside experts.

7. At least one group member should be assigned the role of Devil's advocate to question all the group's ideas. This should be a different person for each meeting.

As a final step to encourage good group decision making, the group should hold a final meeting to give everyone a last chance to choose another course of action.

YOUR TURN

Can you think of situations where you have done things which you would not have done otherwise because you were in a group? Write out one event in your journal or notebook and include the reasons why you think you went along with the group.

MORE FUN

Know your own limits. Setting clear limits for yourself will enable you to be prepared. Ask yourself what you will and will not do in various situations, and write these down in your journal. Will you take drugs? Can you ever be persuaded to do something which is not right for you? In your journal, list as many things as you can think of which are not right for you in one column and your reasons for thinking so in another.

Imagine at least five senarios in which you may be subject to peer pressure. Note these down in your journal in one column, and in a second column next to each scenario write down how you would like yourself to react should such a situation occur.

DID YOU KNOW?

The results of Groupthink can often be disastrous. One example is the Space Shuttle Challenger disaster in 1986. The Challenger broke apart 73 seconds from take off, leading to the deaths of the seven crew members. The pressure not to delay the launch for months overcame the engineering concern for safety. When the final decision to launch was made, select individuals were asked to make a decision verbally and, because of group pressure, the decision was made to launch.

Groupthink can also be seen in some of the uglier historical incidents of the 20th Century: the Rwanda genocide of 1994, the rise of Fascism, Nazism, and Stalinism in Europe in the 1930s. In each case, thousands, if not millions, of people were killed while neighbors refused to go against the groups responsible.

In 1967, a high school history teacher in Palo Alto, California, was unable to explain to his students how so many people in Nazi Germany could claim they were ignorant of what was going on (when between 11 and 17 million people were exterminated, including 6 million Jews) and how so few German citizens resisted. The teacher realized he had no answer which was satisfactory enough, so he started a movement. The book *The Wave* by Todd Strasser is based on this event. Reading it may help you understand more about the power of obedience to authority, peer pressure and the importance of setting your limits clearly before someone pressures you into something (drugs, drinking, sex, or stereotyping).

Foot in the Door (or Nose Under the Tent)

Sometimes peer pressure shows up as a small, seemingly innocent request. There is an old Arabian proverb: "If the camel once gets his nose in the tent, his body will soon follow." And soon the tent poles will be ripped out and the shelter lost.

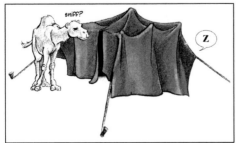

Responding to peer pressure is part of human nature, but some people are more likely to give in, and others are better able to resist and stand their ground. People who are low on confidence and those who tend to follow rather than lead could be more likely to seek their peers' approval by giving in to a risky challenge or suggestion. People who are unsure of themselves, new to the group, or inexperienced with peer pressure may also be more likely to give in.

—HOOKED

Consider this: you and your friends are in the schoolyard and someone starts gossiping about an acquaintance who isn't present. It all begins innocent enough about a silly incident. Before you know it, everyone starts sharing embarrassing incidents or put-downs. You don't really have anything against this person and you probably wouldn't be teasing this much if he/she were present. If you can't resist jumping in or "piling on," you've taken the bait.

How can you recognize when peer pressure is making you consider something which you think is not good for you, and how can you defend yourself? Here are three good ways on how to avoid the hook:

1. **Prevention:** Preventing negative peer pressure is best. If you surround yourself with people who feel and behave the same way you do, you are less likely to get into trouble. It can really help to have at least one other peer, or friend, who is willing to say "no," too. This takes a lot of the power out of peer pressure and makes it much easier to resist. It's great to have friends with values similar to yours who will back you up when you don't want to do something. Friends who will speak up with you when you're in need of moral support can be lifesavers. If you're hearing that little voice telling you a situation's not right, speak up. Chances are others hear it, too. Just having one other person stand with you against peer pressure makes it much easier for both people to resist.

   You've probably had a parent and teacher advise you to "choose your friends wisely." Peer pressure is a big reason why they say this. If you choose friends who don't use drugs, cut class, smoke cigarettes, or lie to their parents or caregivers, then you probably won't do these things either, even if other kids do. Try to help a friend who's having trouble resisting

99

peer pressure. It can be powerful for one kid to join another by simply saying, "I'm with you - let's go."

2. **Avoid Drugs and Alcohol:** You probably have heard the expression "under the influence." It usually refers to using alcohol or drugs, which when mixed with peer pressure, can lead to some very poor decisions. These substances can throw off your judgment and interfere with your ability to think about consequences and make good decisions.

3. **Peer Pressure Reversal:** Peer pressure is just that . . . a pressure on you to act or think in a certain way. The decision about whether to allow yourself to be influenced by peers on important issues is yours. It may not be easy to resist peer pressure. But you can develop the skills to defend yourself.

First you need to recognize peer pressure, then assess it, and finally, escape it.

Family counselor Sharon Scott[11] has developed a useful approach called Peer Pressure Reversal in her book *How to Say No and Keep Your Friends*. We've adapted her 3-step model:

> Step 1: Be a Detective
> Step 2: Be a Judge and Jury
> Step 3: Be an Escape Artist

Let's look more closely at each step.

Step 1: Be a Detective

To resist negative peer pressure, you first have to **recognize when it's happening.** It's not always easy, because it can come disguised as friendly help or a seemingly innocent invitation to have some fun. What are some clues that a good peer pressure detective would look for in a situation where peer pressure is being applied?

Look for Trouble: Scope out the scene. Do you notice anything that seems unusual? Are people whispering secrets or acting suspiciously? Are adults around supervising? Does the location look dangerous? Are there strange or older kids around?

Listen for Trouble: Listen to what others are saying. Are they asking you to do something unusual? Do they say things like "Everyone's doing it," "You're a chicken if you don't do this," or "We won't get caught."

Step 2: Be a Judge and Jury

Once you have collected the evidence, you need to decide on whether to join in or say no. First, it is helpful to consider whether the activity breaks a law. Sometimes you may know, but sometimes you may have to ask. If you don't know if it is illegal (such as skipping school, damaging other's property, making a prank phone call, fighting, using obscene language in public, etc.), then assume it is until you find out otherwise.

Also, consider what a parent, teacher and other adult might say. Is it likely to make them angry or upset?

As a judge, you can consider the pros and the cons of the activity. Ask yourself, "If I do this what good could happen?" and "If I do this, what bad could happen?" Most often peers will exaggerate the good things, and downplay the bad possibilities. You are likely to hear "This will be fun," "It feels so good," "A little won't hurt," etc.

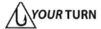 **YOUR TURN**

A friend asks to copy your homework . . . just this once. What good things might come of this if you agree? Make a list. Now what bad things might happen as a result of allowing someone to copy your homework? Be imaginative.

Finally, when you have considered the good and the bad, it's time to reach a verdict. Thumbs up or thumbs down. What does your inner judge tell you and what does your "gut" tell you? Are you likely to regret, feel guilty or try to hide what you are about to do? Those are good clues not to proceed. If you feel uncomfortable, even if your friends seem to be OK with what's going on, it means that something about the situation is wrong for you.

In general, if you are not sure, best to decline the offer and decide not to follow the peer pressure. The more certain and clear you can be, the better. Otherwise, it is likely your friends or peers will keep pestering you and try to get you to change your mind.

Step 3: Be an Escape Artist

So, you have checked out the situation, collected the clues, considered the pros and cons, now it's time to act. And the quicker the better. There are many ways to get out of the situation. You can use your words and your feet to avoid trouble.

Sometimes you can even anticipate trouble and plan ahead of time what you will say and do. If you'd like to go to a party but you believe you may be offered alcohol or drugs there, think ahead about how you'll handle this challenge. Decide ahead of time - and even rehearse - what you'll say and do. Learn a few tricks. If you're holding a bottle of water or a can of soda, for instance, you're less likely to be offered a drink you don't want.

What You Can Say to Escape

■ Just Say No:

This is the simplest, most direct and honest way to respond to undesirable peer pressure. You can say "no" politely or firmly depending on the situation. And there are many, many words to mean "no": "No thanks," "I'll pass on this," "I'd rather not." There are dozens more. Sometimes you may have to repeat your "no" over and over like a broken record until your friend finally gets bored, frustrated and gives up. Don't you give up or give in.

⚠️ YOUR TURN

1. How many ways can you say "no"? Make a list.

2. How many ways can you say "no" with gestures or with body language? Practice each one.

■ Excuse Me:

With good friends you should never have to offer an explanation or apology. A simple "no" should be enough. But if you feel you need an excuse for, say, turning down a drink or smoke, think up a few lines you can use when you need them. You can always say, "No, thanks, I've got a belt test in karate next week and I'm in training," or "No way - my uncle just died of cirrhosis and I'm not even looking at any booze." An excuse may even allow you to decline the offer without having to say "no" directly. Here are a few general-purpose excuses to get you started:

o "I've got other plans."

o "I got to go to _____ (meet someone, sports practice, music lessons) in a few minutes."

o "I've got too much homework to do" or "I haven't finished my homework."

o "I promised I would help with chores (like babysitting, dishes, yard-work, etc.)"

o "It sounds lame, but I have to check with my parents first."

o "I have to make a telephone call."

o "I think I am allergic to it."

o "I tried it once and got caught. I'll never do that again."

o "I really don't like the taste of it."

o "I don't like the way it makes me feel."

Can you add to the list of excuses?

■ Change the Subject:

When someone asks you to do something you don't want to, you can act like you didn't hear what he or she said, make a joke, or distract him or her by changing the subject. Think of something which the person might be really interested in (like sports, clothes, dating, music, movies, and so on). Jump right into a conversation about that hot topic. You might start with: "Did you see _____ (the latest movie, football

105

game, etc.)? What did you think?" Keep the conversation going to avoid falling back on the troubling subject.

Another way to change the subject is to suggest a better idea. You can use positive peer pressure yourself to refocus your friend on safer, legal alternatives. Simply offer: "Hey, I've got a great idea. Let's do this: _____" or "Why don't we _____ instead." You can fill in the blank with any activity which sounds like fun. Doing homework doesn't usually work in this situation, so try playing a sport, listening to some music, calling a friend, grabbing something to eat, and so on. Your excitement or enthusiasm for the alternative will sway the discussion.

What You Can Do to Escape

Probably the most important thing you can do to avoid negative peer pressure and trouble is to walk away. If you find yourself having to say "no" repeatedly, or any of the other escape words don't seem to be working, it's time to leave the scene. The quicker the better. If you try a slow exit, you leave time for others to hassle or try to talk you out of leaving. You need to appear decisive as you exit. You don't necessarily have to give an excuse or explanation. Sometimes a brief "I'm outta here" will do.

 **KEEP IT IN MIND**

When you are faced with negative peer pressure, such as whether or not to take drugs or to drink alcohol, imagine that someone younger than you, your younger brother, sister or cousin, is watching what you are doing. Young children look up to and learn how to behave from their older siblings and the other young adults in their lives. Remembering this when you are faced with a difficult choice can help you make the kinds of decisions that will ensure that you are a good **role model** for the young children around you.

Key Ideas in Chapter 7

The **social-proof principle** states that we often determine what is correct by finding out what other people think is correct. We observe what our **peers** are doing in a situation and tend to act or think in the same manner. That is why parents and teachers often suggest that we choose our friends carefully: friends influence each other.

Social influence has been demonstrated by researchers, such as Stanley Asch, where subjects made incorrect choices to avoid being singled out and rejected by the group. **Peer pressure** to behave in a certain way, or **group influence**, is common for humans of any age and in any society. Although peer pressure can help us make fewer mistakes by acting in accordance with what is accepted or what is in the group's **comfort zone**, it can also be used with serious consequences.

Learning to recognize **negative peer pressure** or **Groupthink** is the first step in preventing bad or harmful behavior or thoughts. Surround yourself with friends who are like you, never mix peer pressure with drugs or alcohol, and learn some prevention methods for getting out of situations where negative peer pressure is being applied. Know when to say no, how to change the subject, and when and how to escape.

⚠ YOUR TURN

Consider each of the following sticky situations, and write in your journal how you would respond. If you get stuck, look back in the chapter to try out some ways to check out the scene, weigh the pros and cons, and then escape the situation with your words and actions.

○ You are staying over at a friend's house and his/her parents are not home. Your friend suggests inviting a bunch of other kids over for a *real* party.

107

○ You have been dating someone for several months. Your partner wants to have sex. He or she says, "Everyone is doing it."

○ You are with a group of friends. They begin to gossip about a class-mate. The classmate walks up and the group begins to tease or bully him or her.

○ You hear that there is a substitute teacher in one of your classes who doesn't usually take attendance. Your friends ask you to cut class with them and go get a bite to eat.

 **KEEP IT IN MIND**

OK, it's not always easy to resist negative peer pressure or to be different. But when you do, it is usually easy to feel good about yourself afterwards. You may even be a positive influence on your peers who feel the same way - often it just takes one person to speak out or take a different action to change a situation. Your friends may follow if you have the courage to do something different or refuse to go along with the group. Remember, just because "everyone is doing it" does not mean it is right. With practice (in other words, 1. Be a Detective; 2. Be a Judge and Jury; and 3. Be an Escape Artist), you can resist the influence of peer pressure.

8

Caught In The Net:
Don't Get Hooked Online

Go onto the internet. Try typing in the name of someone you know in a search engine like Google. Chances are that you'll see a bunch of information pop up. Pictures. Biographies. Do you think the person knows that all this information about him or her is out there and easily available . . . to anybody . . . forever?

WHAT'S GOING ON?

The internet is a fantastic place to hang out. You can stay in touch with friends and family, meet new friends, find information, download music, buy things, check out the latest sports scores, and much more. Yes, the internet is a great place.

Cyberspace is like a giant lake. You can swim, boat, wind-surf, and have fun and meet new people. But sometimes you cannot see beneath the surface. There may be hidden rocks, strong currents, stinging jellyfish, even sharks. There are places you should not swim alone and people you should avoid. Think "Jaws."

Although most people we meet online are there to help us,

109

sadly, there are some who want to meet young people and do them harm. For example, one in five U.S. teenagers who regularly log on to the internet say they have received an unwanted **sexual solicitation** via the web. Sexual solicitations are requests to engage in sexual activities or sexual talk, or to give out personal sexual information. One in 33 youths received an aggressive sexual solicitation in the past year on the 'net. This means a predator asked a young person to meet somewhere, called a young person on the phone, and/or sent the young person correspondence, money, or gifts through the mail. There are other dangers. If you have a credit card number and give it to someone through the internet, that person can "steal your identity" and run up quite a bill on your card.

And it's not just the chat rooms, social networks (like Facebook, Twitter or MySpace), or email on the internet that can be unsafe. Today cellphones can exchange information through texting, voicemail, instant messaging, or by sending photographs. All these can put you in touch with people and places that can make you feel uncomfortable or harm you.

TRY THIS

Take a piece of paper and write on it a note about yourself. Perhaps it contains something secret that you would just want to give to one friend who you will see later. After thinking about it, you decide not to pass on the note and tear it up. It's gone.

Now imagine you wrote that same note in an email or text message to that friend. With a click it is instantly sent. There is no taking it back. No retrieving it.

WHAT'S GOING ON?

It's important to realize that whatever you write or whatever pictures you send, can live forever in cyberspace even if you delete or erase it. The information and images may still be stored, archived and cached on computer storage units somewhere in the world. What you send out can also be copied, forwarded, and shared with one other person, or millions of others. Something which you may have meant to share with or say to only one person, suddenly, in seconds, can be visible to millions. And it lives forever . . . often copied, stored, and can't be erased. This information from and about you can last longer than a tattoo!

What you think is funny today (say it's a photo of yourself or joking about a friend), may not seem so funny if read by others, or viewed 20 years from now. For example, some colleges or employers search the internet for information about applicants and turn up some embarrassing information. Even things you send to friends can be used against you if they become ex-friends. There is no way to take back what you put out in emails, chat rooms, message boards, or instant messages.

DID YOU KNOW?

Online bullying, called **cyberbullying**, happens when teens use the internet, cellphones, or other devices to send or post text or images intended to hurt or embarrass another person. Cyberbullying is a problem which affects almost half of all American teens. The National Crime Prevention Council (NCPC) says:

Being a victim of cyberbullying can be a common and painful experience. Some youth who cyberbully:

o Pretend they are other people online to trick others

o Spread lies and rumors about victims

o Trick people into revealing personal information

o Send or forward cruel text messages

o Post pictures of victims without their consent

When teens were asked why they think others cyberbully, 81% said that cyberbullies think it's funny. Other teens believe that youth who cyberbully:

o Don't think it's a big deal

o Don't think about the consequences

o Are encouraged by friends

o Think everybody cyberbullies

o Think they won't get caught

Victims of cyberbullying experience a variety of emotions when it happens to them - anger, sadness, embarrassment, fear. These emotions can cause victims to react in a number of ways, such as seeking revenge on the bully, perhaps even cyberbullying back (and thus continuing the spread of cyberbullying). Many victims are so upset that they avoid their friends and their social activities, and sometimes suffer much more serious emotional reactions, which can even lead to suicide.

If you feel you are a victim of cyberbullying, the best thing you can do is report it to your parents, teachers or other responsible adults. Ignoring it will not fix the problem.

HOOKED

Suppose you receive an unexpected request on your social network site from a stranger to become friends. This person mentions that he or she is already friends with several people on your friends' list. This person also points out that you two are wearing a similar shirt in your profile picture. This person "bets" that you have a lot in common, and you seem a lot more interesting than some of the other people on this site. Oh BTW - this person is going away for the weekend so it would be great to hear from you soon. "Can't wait!" If you confirm this request without checking with your other friends about this person's identity, you've taken the bait.

AVOID THE HOOK

So, how can you have fun, meet people, get information, and yet remain safe in cyberspace? Fortunately, there are a few tips which can really help:

1. Know Who You Are Communicating With

People online may not be who you think they are. Let's say you visit a chat room for teens only. You begin a conversation with a nice girl. She says she is 14 and goes to a neighboring school. She loves horses, she has twin younger brothers who play soccer. She

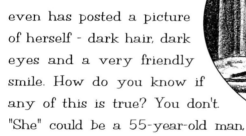

even has posted a picture of herself - dark hair, dark eyes and a very friendly smile. How do you know if any of this is true? You don't. "She" could be a 55-year-old man, with gray whiskers, an addiction to alcohol and young boys. This happens. You simply cannot know who is really behind the messages.

A famous cartoon from the magazine *The New Yorker* shows a dog sitting in front of a computer telling another dog, "On the internet, nobody knows you're a dog." Of course, this might have to be a dog who could type!

If you do get an email, photograph, or response in a chat room which embarrasses you, makes you feel uncomfortable, or is offensive, do not respond back. Let your parent or another adult know. This will help protect you and your friends.

2. Don't Get Personal

Since you may not know who you are interacting with, or who might be reading or viewing what you are saying, don't give out any personal information. This includes your:

- o Full name
- o Home address
- o Phone number
- o Social security number
- o Passwords
- o Names of family members
- o Credit card numbers

It's easy to see how such information could be harmful if it falls into the wrong hands. But sometimes it is more subtle.

⚠ YOUR TURN

Let's say you are in a chat room on someone's MySpace page. There is a picture of that person wearing a high school sweatshirt and the person writes:

"Oh, I just love the Border's bookstore CD collection. My friend Sally Buttons and I are looking forward to going there for the big sale that starts on Saturday. I can't wait to buy The Decemberists' latest CD."

Do you think you could locate this person and arrange to meet him/her secretly? What were the clues?

There are lots of ways people can lure personal information out of you and manipulate you on the internet. For example, can you match the "hook" or "bait" in each of these examples with the risk or problem it might cause?

The Hook or Bait	The Problem
1. "Let's go private."	a. You didn't give your telephone number, or did you? With caller ID, just calling someone gives him/her your telephone number and can open yourself to unwanted calls, contact or harassment.
2. "Who's your favorite band, clothing maker, film, etc."	
3. "I know someone who can get you a modeling job."	b. Flattery. Asking for photos and promising modeling can be a lead-in to a personal meeting.

4. "I know a way you can earn money fast."	c. Knowing what you really like, the person can offer you gifts like concert tickets, CDs, etc., but sometimes at the cost of your safety.
5. "My computer isn't working well. Why not call me on my cellphone so we can continue to chat?"	d. Leaving a public chat room to do private chat, instant messaging, or phone texting may be an invitation to trouble.
	e. Making a personal, emotional connection with a stranger.
6. "You sound sad. Tell me what's troubling you."	f. If an offer seems too good to be true, it probably is just an attempt to get personal information.

Answers: 1 (d), 2 (c), 3 (b), 4 (f), 5 (a), 6 (e). How did you do?

There are other ways people can pry personal information out of you. One is called **phishing**. It involves contacting you (by phone or email) and asking for sensitive information such as usernames, passwords and credit card details while masquerading as a trustworthy source. For example, you may get an official looking email saying that your password needs to be changed to allow you to continue to send and receive emails. The email has a link to click on which takes you to a false website that looks similar to the real email site. There you

117

might be asked for your name, password or other personal information. The people at the other end of this fraud can then use this information to access your accounts. Don't take the bait.

3. Don't Meet in Person

Probably the most dangerous thing which can come from the internet is when you agree to meet an "online friend" in person. You don't really know who will show up for the meeting. Sometimes he or she can mean you harm. If you are even considering meeting someone you met only on the 'net (please don't), at least don't go alone (more is merrier), don't meet in a private place, and don't go without discussing with a parent or adult.

4. Remember Online Information is Forever

Before you send or post something, ask yourself if there is anyone now or in the future you would not want to read or see what you send. If so, think before you send. There is no way to take back what you put out in emails, chat rooms, message boards, or instant messages.

The internet and cellphones are wonderful tools, if you know how to avoid getting caught in the net.

http://staysafeonline.org/ is an excellent site. Among other things, it lists useful guidelines for the "Thoughtful and Safe Digital Citizen" and lists resources for information on and prevention of cyberbullying.

Key Ideas in Chapter 8

While most people you meet online are there to help, there are some who want to meet young people and do them harm. One in five U.S. teenagers who regularly log on to the internet has received an unwanted **sexual solicitation** via the web.

Follow simple rules to avoid getting hooked or hurt: Know who you are communicating with; never agree to meet with an "online friend" you don't really know; and never give out personal information about yourself or others, especially credit card numbers. **Cyberbullying** is a trend that affects over half of American teens today; learning ways to prevent it and how to report it to responsible adults will help lessen emotional consequences. Think about what you post online or send via cellphone or email because it can last forever with millions reading or seeing it.

 **KEEP IT IN MIND**

The influence techniques discussed in this book often work because of the way our brain works when making judgments. Review the main ideas of each chapter from time to time so you can keep them in mind. Share these ideas with friends and continue to try to identify the influence techniques being used whenever you go shopping.

But, remember, these techniques can be used anywhere - especially where you least expect it. Review the scenario in the above Hooked section. How many influence techniques can you identify in that person's pitch to become your friend?

Summary

Remember the fish which got more than it bargained for by snapping onto the lure? (See page 8.) It did this out of instinct. But, what if the fish had been taught that sometimes things are not what they seem? Do you think it would have snapped so quickly, or would it have looked closer and noticed the hook?

Because we are bombarded daily by advertisers telling us to buy now before it's gone, by authorities telling us what we can or cannot do, and by our friends and relations telling us everyone else is doing it, we can understand how hard it is to be alert to our own needs and our own good sense. More and more, advertisers and marketers are coming up with new and clever ways to get you hooked.

Remember the "Which is the better deal?" question on page 20? If you answered that 25% off one T-shirt was a better deal because you wouldn't be paying full price PLUS an additional 50% for a second shirt, you will be happy to know that you can't easily be hooked by tricky advertising. (Of course, if you needed to buy two shirts, then either deal would be a good choice.)

Take time to examine your needs and how you can obtain them without getting overloaded by outside influences. Trust your warning flags, because in many cases, it means "Beware . . . there's a hook in there somewhere!"

Activities for Teachers to Use in the Classroom

1. Divide the class into groups. Give each group a picture of a product (sneakers, car, stereo system). Tell each team the cost of their item and make the costs different amounts (some very inexpensive, some expensive). Then have them rate the quality of the product (scale of 1 to 10 with 1 being lowest).

Discussion: Discuss the ratings each group gives to their product, and see if people tend to assume that higher prices mean higher quality.

2. Writing task: Videogame devices often sell for close to or less than they cost to manufacture, distribute, and market. Have the students find newspaper or magazine ads where stuff is practically given away. Then, have them write about why they think companies can afford to "give products away." Have them calculate the real cost of the product. For example, if an inkjet printer is sold for $49 but the color ink cartridges sell for $12 each and you have to replace all 4 cartridges at least 4 times a year, how much do you end up paying to the company in 3 years?

3. Play-acting task: Suppose you wanted the person sitting next to you to like you more. Using the principles discussed in the book, how could you arrange your next encounter to accomplish your goal? Divide the class into groups, and assign each group the task of making up a short play (5-10 mins.) about this problem, and present it to the class.

Discussion: After the presentations, have each group discuss the principles used in the presentations.

4. Divide the class into groups. Give them all the same essay (on any subject) to review, discuss and grade. Attach a photograph of an attractive or unattractive person to each essay. See if the average "grade" is influenced by the photographs.

Discussion: Have each group discuss the principles involved in the choices.

5. Let's say the class works for an advertising company. Divide the class into groups and ask each group to develop an ad campaign to promote a new food product (you pick one). Tell them to use as many tools of influence as they can to design the campaign to promote sales of their product.

6. Divide the class into groups. Have them design a television commercial, again using the tools of influence, to try to prevent the use of cigarettes by teenagers.
Discussion: Have each group discuss using tools of influence for good causes, as well as for bad.

7. Select a rock or hip-hop video or an ad from a teenage-demographic magazine. Have the students list the ways in which the tools of influence are used to "hook" the viewer/reader.

8. It is now common to be offered the opportunity to "supersize" your meal for just a small increase in price. Explain how the tools of influence can be used to sell "supersizing."
Discussion: Discuss how this can be helpful or harmful to people.
Suggestions: Discuss health problems in the USA which may have a connection to this philosophy of "supersizing."

9. Organize a classroom cookie sale. Have the baked goods separated on the table in plates. On one larger plate, place a sign saying "Special Chocolate Chip Cookies (or some other kind): 2 for 10 cents." All the other cookies on the table will be sold for 5 cents each, but with no special sign. The students will then observe and write down how many customers buy from the plate with the Special sign. Instruct the students that they are not to discuss the experiment with their customer so that they can keep the results unbiased. Then, they should write down how many buy from the Special plate and how many say "Hey, that's no bargain!"

Discussion: Why would people prefer to purchase at exactly the same price or even at higher prices just because of signs and advertising.

Follow-up: Have the students decide where to spend the money made from the sale. You, as their teacher, should make suggestions. After their decision, have the students write a paragraph on how they made the decision on spending the money. Were they influenced by you, the authority figure, or by something else?

10. Writing task: Have the students make up a story about influence. They can write about someone being influenced by another or about others doing the influencing. Once the stories are done, ask for a show of hands of those who wrote from the viewpoint of the victim of influence or from the viewpoint of the influencer.

Discussion: Discuss the finding of this survey. Why do you think there are more people who are influenced than there are those who do the influencing? You may want to collect the stories and use them in other situations where appropriate, such as in health classes where smoking, drugs and harmful behavior are being discussed.

Activities for Understanding Groupthink and Cliques and Gangs

To help students understand more about cliques or gangs and the theory of Groupthink, the following activities from this website will be useful:

http://www.lessonplanspage.com/SSODoSomethingAboutSchool
ViolenceUnitDay5Groupthink912.htm

(1) Tell students to form groups. Allow them to work together to develop a group name, a symbol for their group, and a set of rules their group follows.

(2) Once students have finished their group work, have them reflect on the roles they played within the group. Who was the major

decision-maker? Was there any disagreement among members of the group? How was it resolved?

(3) Remind students that people act differently in group settings. Sometimes they find themselves in a situation which they might not be comfortable with, but for the sake of the group, they follow along.

(4) Ask students whether they think people are more or less likely to be violent when they are in a group setting. Discuss the students' answers.

(5) Share and discuss each of the symptoms that are indicative of Groupthink (refer to page 93 for the list of Janis' eight symptoms). Ask students to think about if they have ever seen examples of Groupthink occurring in their own lives.

Activities for Helping Students Understand About Gangs:

(6) Relate Groupthink to gang mentality. Conduct a discussion on how Groupthink influences gang behavior.

(7) Ask students in pairs to list the reasons why people join gangs. Share these with the class and discuss how a gang is different from just a group of friends.

(8) Share some gang information with students:
- o Gangs are usually defined as a "group of individuals who share a common identity and, in current usage, engage in illegal activities. Once an urban problem, street gangs have now infiltrated U.S. communities large and small. Gang experts say at least 21,500 gangs - with more than 731,000 members - are active nationwide." See the website: **http://staff.lib.msu.edu/harris23/crimjust/gangs.htm**

o Studies which have compared at-risk teens with teenagers in gangs show that the latter group is more likely to be involved with violent crimes.

o Factors which can increase gang involvement are: poverty, divorced families, alcohol and drug abuse, family history of gang involvement, an "us against them" mentality, and previous violent and anti-social behavior.

(9) Have the students, with your assistance, fill out the gang survey on this website - **http://www.gwcinc.com/gguide.htm** - to help them determine if gangs are a problem in their school.

(10) Students can then determine what kind of response would be helpful to decrease gang membership in their school. What could the school do? The community? See the following website for further information:

http://digitalcommons.unl.edu/cgi/viewcontent.cgi?article= 1564&context=extensionhist

(11) Have students write and present their own anti-gang rap.

Additional Activities:

o Ask students to discuss the most violent movies, videogames, songs they have heard or seen. Is it OK to expose people to this violence? Should children be able to see this, too? Do they think this violence influences their behavior? Why or why not?

o **Groupthink Quiz:** a questionnaire which may help you and your students evaluate what they have understood about Groupthink can be found on this link:

http://www.abacon.com/commstudies/groups/groupthinkquiz.html

Glossary of Terms

apathy, a lack of concern for others (or for oneself) in stressful events.

automatic responses, emotional or physical reactions to events in our environment

bias, an attitude or judgment which is influenced by a prejudice against people and interferes with the ability to be impartial.

brainwashing, a form of coercion used to change your way of thinking to something that may be the opposite of what you thought before.

cohesiveness (in a group), how well members in a group are consistent with the rules of that group.

collectibles, items that sellers claim you should collect usually at high prices, but may or may not be rare.

comfort zone (in a group), a group's perceived set of norms which members of the group try not to disrupt in order to maintain the sense of belonging.

comparison effect (or automatic comparison effect), we judge whatever is in our mind at present by comparing it to what happened before. For example, there is the illusion that something is a bargain because you compare it to what has happened before, not on the real value.

compliance, the tendency to go along with something because someone asks us to.

conformity, behavior induced by social influence, and determined by group unanimity, group size, and a person's relationship to others in the group. **Pressure to conform**, feeling the need to do what others are doing.

127

consistency, the act of remaining committed to a belief, a promise, an idea or ideas, and maintaining these views even in cases where the idea or belief is incorrect or unethical.

critical evaluator (in a group), someone who helps to assess other opinions and thoughts on a group's activities.

cults, a group of people who believe in and behave outside the normal accepted behavior of others, often in a much more unhealthy way. Cult leaders are usually charismatic and sometimes unscrupulous persons with a personal motivation to gather followers.

cyberbullying, happens when people use the internet, cellphones, or other devices to send or post text or images intended to hurt or embarrass another person.

deadline tactic, placing an expiration time limit on a product so that we think we have to buy now and not later.

gift exchange, sociologist Georg Simmel's term for the principle of give-and-take (*see below*).

group influence, a tactic of controlling our behavior through establishing norms, roles, and cohesiveness in a group. (*see also* peer pressure).

group rules, *see* norms.

group unanimity, a belief that all members of the group agree with every activity, purpose and rule of the group, which often results in not allowing dissenting or other viewpoints.

Groupthink, the name psychologists give to the type of thinking group members jointly arrive at.

influencer, the person, principle or action that causes us to react in certain ways.

limited-number principle, the selling of a product by advertising its limited quantity, making it seem more desirable.

loss leader, a tactic where a seller will advertise an item at a substantial savings only to entice people to come in pursuit of it and hopefully buy another full-priced item.

Milgram experiment, the experiment carried out by Dr. Stanley Milgram in 1974 to show how people will blindly follow instructions from an authority figure, even at the point of inflicting severe punishment and pain.

mood, relatively longer lasting states of feeling. A mood can set up how one reacts and feels during an experience; for instance, a person in a good mood will more likely help others than one who is in a bad mood.

mood swing, rapidly going from one state of feeling to another more short-term, perhaps opposite feeling.

nonverbal signals, signals used to convey a feeling, such as laughter or face and body movements.

norms (in a group), rules of behavior for a group.

obdience-to-authority theory, normal, healthy individuals are willing to carry out activities such as inflicting severe levels of pain rather than go against "authority." (*see* Milgram experiment)

peer pressure, influence from others in your age group to think and behave in ways the group considers the norm or appropriate for your role in the group; positive peer pressure tends to influence in ways that are helpful to you and the group; negative peer pressure tends to lead to inappropriate or dangerous choices with more serious consequences.

peers, people who are similar to you in your life. (*see also*, peer pressure *and* group influence)

phishing, a fraudulent contact, usually by phone or email, asking for sensitive information such as usernames, passwords and credit card details while masquerading as a trustworthy source.

precious mistake, a flaw in merchandise that makes it more valuable, such as when a postage stamp is misprinted.

principle of give and take, anthropologist Bronislaw Malinowski's term for why we feel obligated to return a favor when someone gives us something. (*see also*, reciprocity rule)

principle of supply and demand, if supply is greater than demand, the price goes down.

product placement, merchandise that is placed subtly in a movie or TV program as a form of subliminal advertising.

programmed or programming, the automatic way we respond to influences or stimuli based on what we have learned.

reciprocity rule, also known as the **gift-giving principle**, says a gift, no matter how small or large, must be reciprocated (returned as a favor), and that larger gifts make this rule even more powerful.

reference group, the group that people choose to compare themselves to.

reflex obligation, the feeling that you must buy something or accept something simply because someone has given you a gift or done a favor for you ... you feel obliged to do it.

reflexive emotional response or **reaction**, a feeling of excitement and arousal as a reaction to a stimulus (or an event). These reactions seem to be due to how our brains are wired to respond.

role (within a group), an assigned task or understood placement within a group, such as being the leader, the group clown, etc.

role model, a person who others look up to for guidance and for modeling their own behavior. Many younger children will look to their older siblings as their role models.

scarcity phenomenon, we tend to value things more when we think they are scarce or rare. For example, a marketing ploy may deliberately cause a product to be scarce, or simply indicate that it is scarce, in order to entice people to want it.

sexual solicitation (on the internet), online requests to engage in unwanted activities, such as sexual talk, or requests to giving out personal sexual information.

social influence, the pressure or sway toward a behavior caused by those in authority or from peer pressure.

social-proof principle, making decisions based on the principle that if others are doing something, it's OK for us to do so, too.

status symbol, an outward symbol, like clothing, cars, jewelry, furniture, houses, etc., that people use to show their perceived authority or superiority.

stealth marketing, the tactic whereby advertisers promote their products using subtle and hidden ways that entice people without their knowing it.

theory of consistency and commitment, the theory that people will remain committed to something because of their need to be consistent

trait, a personality characteristic, such as being conservative or liberal, timid or tough-minded.

References

1. Asch, Solomon E., Studies of independence and conformity: A minority of one against a unanimous majority. *Psychological Monographs, 70*(9, Whole No. 416), 1956.

2. Festinger, Leon, A theory of social comparison processes. *Human Relations, 7,* 117-140, 1954.

3. Freedman, J. L., & Fraser, S. C., Compliance Without Pressure: The Foot-In-The-Door Technique, *Journal of Personality and Social Psychology, 4,* 195-202, 1966.

4. Giedd, J. N., Lalonde, F. M., Celano, M. J., White, S. L., Wallace, G. L., Lee, N. R., Lenroot, R. K., Anatomical brain magnetic resonance imaging of typically developing children and adolescents. *Journal of the American Academy of Child & Adolescent Psychiatry. 48*(5):465-70. 2009.

5. Janis, Irving, *Groupthink (2nd ed.).* Wadsworth Publishing, 1982.

6. Malinowski, Bronislaw, *Crime and Customs in Savage Society.* Littlefield Adams, 1985.

7. Milgram, Stanley, Behavioral study of obedience. *Journal of Abnormal and Social Psychology, 67,* 371-378 (1963). *See also,* Milgram. S., *Obedience to Authority: An Experimental View.* Harper Perennial Modern Classics; Reprint edition, 2009.

8. Newcomb, T.M., Koenig, K.E., Flacks, R., Warwick, D.P., and others, *Persistence and Change: Bennington College and its Students After Twenty-Five Years.* Wiley (1967).

9. Ohio State University (2003, July 8). Nodding or shaking your head may even influence your own thoughts. *ScienceDaily*. (see: http://www.sciencedaily.com/releases/2003/07/030708092002.htm)

10. Regan, Dennis T., Effects of a favor and liking on compliance, *Journal of Experimental Social Psychology*, 7, 627-639 (1971).

11. Scott, Sharon, *How to Say No and Keep Your Friends: Peer Pressure Reversal for Teens and Preteens*. Human Resource Development Press, 1997.

12. Simmel, Georg, & Wolff, K.H., ed., *The Sociology of Georg Simmel*. Free Press (1964).

13. Worchel, S., Lee, J., & Adewole, A., Effects of supply and demand on ratings of object value. *Journal of Personality and Social Psychology*, 32, 906-914 (1975).

14. Zimbardo, Philip G. Stanford Prison Experiment: A Simulation Study of the Psychology of Imprisonment Conducted at Stanford University, official site: http://www.prisonexp.org/. *See also*, Zimbardo, P.G., *The Lucifer Effect: Understanding How Good People Turn Evil*. Random House, 2007.

Website References

http://www.loni.ucla.edu/~esowell/edevel/pub.html - Listing of brain development imaging research papers by Elizabeth Sowell and the UCLA Neuro Imaging Lab

http://www.prisonexp.org/ - Details and videos of the Stanford Prison Experiment.

http://staysafeonline.org/ - Guidelines and key ideas for online safety, published by National Cyber Security Alliance, 1010 Vermont Ave. NW, Suite 821 Washington, DC 20005.

http://www.lessonplanspage.com/SSODoSomethingAboutSchoolViolence UnitDay5Groupthink912.htm - Information about cliques or gangs and the theory of Groupthink, including a list of lesson plans around this subject, published by Hot Chalk, Inc., 1999 S. Bascom Avenue, Suite 1020, Campbell, CA 95008.

http://staff.lib.msu.edu/harris23/crimjust/gangs.htm - Information and data on gangs in America, compiled by Michigan State University Libraries, Criminal Justice and Social Sciences Collections, 100 Library, E. Lansing, MI 48824-1048.

http://www.gwcinc.com/gguide.htm - gang survey to determine if gangs are a problem in a school, published by GWC, Inc., P.O. Box 5023, 530 Falling Springs Road, Cahokia, IL 62206.

http://digitalcommons.unl.edu/cgi/viewcontent.cgi?article=1564&context=extensionhist - Information on how schools and community can decrease or prevent gang membership, published by University of Nebraska-Lincoln, CIT, Lincoln, NE 68583-0918.

http://www.abacon.com/commstudies/groups/groupthinkquiz.html - A questionnaire to evaluate what students understand about Groupthink, by Tim Borchers, Moorhead State University, ©1999 Allyn & Bacon.

http://www.ncpc.org/cyberbullying - Information on cyberbullying from National Crime Prevention Council (NCPC). It contains links to websites to help with prevention and education on the subject.

Further Reading

Cialdini, Robert B., *Influence: Science and Practice, 5th edition*. Allyn & Bacon, 2009.

Covey, Sean, *The Seven Habits of Highly Effective Teens*, Franklin Covey Co., 1998 (published by Simon & Schuster).

Goldstein, Noah J., Martin, Steve J., and Cialdini, Robert B., *Yes! 50 Scientifically Proven Ways to Be Persuasive*. Free Press, 2008.

Janis, Irving, *Groupthink (2nd ed.)*. Wadsworth Publishing, 1982.

Ornstein, Robert, and Ehrlich, Paul, *New World New Mind*, Malor Books, 2000.

Ornstein, Robert, and Carstensen, Laura, *Psychology: The Study of Human Experience, Third Edition*, Harcourt Brace Jovanovich, 1991.

Scott, Sharon, *How to Say No and Keep Your Friends: Peer Pressure Reversal for Teens and Preteens*. Human Resource Development Press, 1997.

Shah, Idries, *The Pleasantries of the Incredible Mulla Nasrudin*, The Estate of Idries Shah, 1983 (distributed in the U.S. by ISHK Book Service).

Strasser, Todd, *The Wave*. Laurel Leaf Publishers, 1981.

Index

American Psychological Association National Standards for High School Psychology Curricula

	Ch. 2: The Comparison Effect	Ch. 3: Give and Take	Ch. 4: Mirror, Mirror	Ch. 5: Scarcity	Ch. 6: Authority	Ch. 7: Peer Pressure	Ch. 8: Caught in the Net
I. METHODS DOMAIN							
• Standard Area IA: Introduction and Research Methods							
CONTENT STANDARD IA-5: Ethical issues in research with human and other animals that are important to psychologists							
IA-5.1 Identify ethical issues in psychological research.							
a. Identify ethical issues in psychological research by discussing ethical issues in psychological research					X		
b. Identify historical examples of research that may have departed from contemporary ethical standards					X		
II. BIOPSYCHOLOGICAL DOMAIN							
• Standard Area IIA: Biological Bases of Behavior							
CONTENT STANDARD IIA-7: How psychological mechanisms are explained by evolution							
IIA-7.1 Explain how evolved tendencies interact with the present environment and culture to determine behavior.							
a. Describe how the environment selects traits and behaviors that increase the survival rate of organisms	X	X		X			
• Standard Area IIB: Sensation and Perception							
CONTENT STANDARD IIB-1: Basic concepts explaining the capabilities and limitations of sensory processes							
IIB-1.4 Relate knowledge of sensory processes to applications in areas such as engineering psychology, advertising, music, architecture, etc.							
a. Analyze advertisements for their use of sensory information			X	X		X	
CONTENT STANDARD IIB-2: Interaction of the person and the environment in determining perception							
IIB-2.3 Describe the influence on perception of environmental variables, motivation, past experiences, culture, and expectations.							
b. Hypothesize why students from different schools disagree about an official's call in a football game			X				
d. Hypothesize about how perceptual principles may relate to stereotypes and prejudice			X			X	
• Standard Area IIC: Motivation and Emotion							
CONTENT STANDARD IIC-1: Motivational concepts							
IIC-1.1 Apply motivational concepts to the behavior of humans and other animals.							
a. Describe their own motives, goals, and values		X				X	
c. Identify the values or motives appealed to in political campaigns or television advertisements	X	X		X	X		
CONTENT STANDARD IIC-7: Effects of motivation and emotion on perception, cognition, and behavior							
IIC-7.2 Explain how learning, memory, problem solving, and decision-making strategies are influenced by motivation and emotion.							
c. Gather examples of advertisements or political appeals designed to motivate choice or behavior	X	X		X	X		
IV. COGNITIVE DOMAIN							
• Standard Area IVA: Learning							
CONTENT STANDARD IVA-3: Principles of operant conditioning							
IVA-3.1 Describe the operant conditioning paradigm.							
a. Describe how consequences influence behavior, such as reinforcement strengthening a behavior's occurrence					X		
b. Identify consequences of punishment in controlling behavior					X		

American Psychological Association National Standards for High School Psychology Curricula
(cont'd.)

	Ch. 2: The Comparison Effect	Ch. 3: Give and Take	Ch. 4: Mirror, Mirror	Ch. 5: Scarcity	Ch. 6: Authority	Ch. 7: Peer Pressure	Ch. 8: Caught in the Net
IV. COGNITIVE DOMAIN (CONT'D.)							
• **Standard Area IVE: Individual Differences**							
CONTENT STANDARD IVE-2: Influence and interaction of heredity and environment on individual differences							
IVE-2.1 Explain how intelligence and personality may be influenced by heredity and environment.							
e. Explaining the role of cultural and group norms in establishing the frames of reference we use in thinking about individual differences	X				X		
V. VARIATIONS IN INDIVIDUAL AND GROUP BEHAVIOR DOMAIN							
• **Standard Area VC: Social and Cultural Dimensions of Behavior**							
CONTENT STANDARD VC-1: Social judgment and attitudes							
VC-1.1 Demonstrate an understanding of person perception.							
a. Explaining the role of social schemas in person perception	X				X		
b. Stating how different kinds of physical attractiveness can influence perceptions of other personal characteristics	X						
c. Describing how cultural socialization determines social schema development	X				X		
VC-1.3 Identify sources of attitude formation.							
a. Providing learning-based interpretations of attitude formation (e.g., Asch)				X			
b. Explaining the role of expectations and stereotyped thinking as they relate to attitude and behavior (e.g., Milgram)				X			
c. Discussing the contribution of role-playing to attitude formation (e.g., Zimbardo's prison experiment)				X			
VC-1.4 Assess some methods used to change attitudes.							
a. Citing research on the effects of advertising and persuasion	X	X			X		
b. Hypothesizing about the potential of media to influence positive attitude change	X				X		
CONTENT STANDARD VC-2: Social and cultural categories							
VC-2.1 Identify basic social and cultural categories.							
b. Describing the components of culture (e.g., symbols, language, norms, and values)					X	X	
CONTENT STANDARD VC-3: Social influence and relationships							
VC-3.1 Describe effects of the presence of others on individual behavior.							
c. Distinguishing differences in social behavior among individuals relative to their exercise of power (e.g., persons with less power may show greater awareness of persons with more power)					X	X	
VC-3.3 Explore the nature and effects of bias and discrimination.							
a. Describing how social biases create a world where one kind of person is considered to be normative, and other kinds of persons are "different" (e.g., males are normative, whereas females are different)	X				X	X	
b. Examining how bias and discrimination influence behavior			X			X	
e. Exploring the nature of in-group/out-group dynamics					X	X	
VC-3.4 Describe circumstances under which conformity and obedience are likely to occur.							
a. Explaining the importance of group size as a predictor of conformity					X	X	
b. Discussing why obedience to authority is a common phenomenon					X		
d. Analyzing disasters from the perspective of the groupthink hypothesis (e.g., space shuttle disaster, Bay of Pigs						X	

California Middle School and High School Health Standards
(Based on the California Framework)

	Ch. 2: The Comparison Effect	Ch. 3: Give and Take	Ch. 4: Mirror, Mirror	Ch. 5: Scarcity	Ch. 6: Authority	Ch. 7: Peer Pressure	Ch. 8: Caught in the Net
Unifying Idea: Acceptance of personal responsibility for lifelong health **Expectation 1:** Students will demonstrate ways in which they can enhance and maintain their health and well-being. **Mental and emotional health:** • Demonstrating personal characteristics that contribute to self-confidence & self-esteem, e.g…responsibility/respect for the dignity of others.	X	X	X	X	X	X	X
• Avoiding self-destructive behaviors and practicing strategies for resisting negative peer pressure.				X		X	X
• Identify risk factors for negative behaviors and develop effective strategies for counteracting these risk factors.	X	X				X	X
Expectation 3: Students will practice behaviors that reduce the risk of becoming involved in potentially dangerous situations and react to potentially dangerous situations in ways that help to protect their health. **Potentially dangerous situations:** • Demonstrating how peers can help each other avoid or cope with potentially dangerous situations in healthy ways.						X	
• Using appropriate skills to avoid, resolve, and cope with conflicts						X	
• Reporting or obtaining assistance when faced with unsafe situations						X	X
• Avoiding, recognizing, and responding to negative social influences and pressure to use alcohol, tobacco, or other drugs.						X	
• Avoiding, recognizing, and responding to negative social influences and pressure to become sexually active, including applying refusal skills when appropriate.						X	
• Recognize and avoid situations that can increase risk of abuse.						X	X
Unifying Idea: Respect for and promotion of the health of others **Expectation 5:** Students will understand and demonstrate how to promote positive health practices within the school and community, including how to cultivate positive relationships with their peers. **Friendship and peer relationships:** • Demonstrating how to resist negative peer pressure.			X			X	
• Encouraging healthy behavior and discouraging unhealthy risk-taking, including strategies for influencing others to avoid the use of alcohol, tobacco, and other drugs as well as other negative behaviors.						X	
• Interact effectively with many different people, including males & females and members of different ethnic and cultural groups.				X			
Unifying Idea: An understanding of the process of growth and development **Expectation 7:** Students will understand and accept individual differences in growth and development. **Growth and Development:** • Demonstrating an understanding of individual differences.	X		X				
• Recognizing health, nutrition, and psychological problems associated with not having a realistic body image, including dieting and eating disorders, and seeking appropriate help.	X						

California Middle School and High School Health Standards
(Based on the California Framework)
(cont'd.)

	Ch. 2: The Comparison Effect	Ch. 3: Give and Take	Ch. 4: Mirror, Mirror	Ch. 5: Scarcity	Ch. 6: Authority	Ch. 7: Peer Pressure	Ch. 8: Caught in the Net
Unifying Idea: Informed use of health-related information, products, and services **Expectation 9:** Students will identify information, products, and services that may be helpful or harmful to their health. **Products and Services:** • Identifying a variety of consumer influences and analyzing how those influences affect decisions.	X	X	X	X	X		
• Using critical-thinking skills to analyze marketing and advertising techniques and their influence on the selection of health-related services and products.		X					
• Using unit pricing to determine the most economical purchases.	X			X			

Web Source: http://www.cde.ca.gov/ci/cr/cf/documents/healthfw.pdf

California State High School Life Science Standards

	Ch. 2: The Comparison Effect	Ch. 3: Give and Take	Ch. 4: Mirror, Mirror	Ch. 5: Scarcity	Ch. 6: Authority	Ch. 7: Peer Pressure	Ch. 8: Caught in the Net
6. Stability in an ecosystem is a balance between competing effects. As a basis for understanding this concept:							
6.a. Students know biodiversity is the sum total of different kinds of organisms and is affected by alterations of habitats.					X		
6.b. Students know how to analyze changes in an ecosystem resulting from changes in climate, human activity, introduction of nonnative species, or changes in population size.					X		
9. As a result of the coordinated structures and functions of organ systems, the internal environment of the human body remains relatively stable (homeostatic) despite changes in the outside environment.							
9.b. The nervous system mediates communication	X	X	X	X			

Web Source: http://www.cde.ca.gov/ci/cr/cf/documents/scienceframework.pdf

National Board for Professional Teaching Standards - Health

(These standards are for teachers who are attempting
to become board certified. This curricula for *What's the Catch?* falls in
line with methods teachers can use to show their competency)

	Ch. 2: The Comparison Effect	Ch. 3: Give and Take	Ch. 4: Mirror, Mirror	Ch. 5: Scarcity	Ch. 6: Authority	Ch. 7: Peer Pressure	Ch. 8: Caught in the Net
I. Knowledge of Students Accomplished health education teachers obtain a clear understanding of individual students, their family structures, and their backgrounds.	X	X	X	X	X	X	X
II. Knowledge of Subject Matter Accomplished health education teachers have a deep understanding of the components of health and health content and their interrelationships.	X	X	X	X	X	X	X
III. Promoting Skills-Based Learning Accomplished health education teachers, through their passion and effective communication, maintain and improve health-enhancing student behavior by delivering health content through skills-based learning.	X	X	X	X	X	X	X
IV. Curricular Choices Accomplished health education teachers select, plan, adapt, and evaluate curriculum to ensure comprehensive health education.	X	X	X	X	X	X	X
V. Instructional Approaches Accomplished health education teachers use an array of engaging instructional strategies to facilitate student learning.	X	X	X	X	X	X	X

Web Source: http://www.nbpts.org/userfiles/File/Health_53_STD.pdf

National Board Professional Teaching Standard: Adolescence and Young Adulthood Science Standards

(These standards represent how *What's the Catch?* can aid a teacher's pursuit in helping students achieve science literacy as described by the National Department of Education)

	Hits Standard Well	Touches on Standard
Preparing the Way for Productive Student Learning **I. Understanding Students** Accomplished Adolescence and Young Adulthood Science teachers know how students learn, know their students as individuals, and determine students' understanding of science as well as their individual learning backgrounds.		X
II. Understanding Science Accomplished Adolescence and Young Adulthood Science teachers have a broad and current knowledge of science and science education, along with in-depth knowledge of one of the subfields of science, which they use to set important and appropriate learning goals.		X
III. Understanding Science Teaching Accomplished Adolescence and Young Adulthood Science teachers employ a deliberately sequenced variety of research-driven instructional strategies and select, adapt, and create instructional resources to support active student exploration and understanding of science.	X	
Establishing a Favorable Context for Student Learning **IV. Engaging the Science Learner** Accomplished Adolescence and Young Adulthood Science teachers spark student interest in science and promote active and sustained learning, so all students achieve meaningful and demonstrated growth toward learning goals.		X
Advancing Student Learning **VII. Fostering Science Inquiry** Accomplished Adolescence and Young Adulthood Science teachers engage students in active exploration to develop the mental operations and habits of mind that are essential to advancing strong content knowledge and scientific literacy.		X
VIII. Making Connection in Science Accomplished Adolescence and Young Adulthood Science teachers create opportunities for students to examine the human contexts of science, including its history, reciprocal relationship with technology, ties to mathematics, and impacts on society, so that students make connections across the disciplines of science, among other subject areas, and in their lives.	X	

Web Source: www.nbpts.org/the_standards/standards_by_cert?ID=4&x=44&y=6

Breinigsville, PA USA
08 November 2010
248925BV00003B/1/P

9 781933 779782